First World War
and Army of Occupation
War Diary
France, Belgium and Germany

4 DIVISION
Divisional Troops
526 Field Company Royal Engineers
18 September 1915 - 28 February 1919

WO95/1470/2

The Naval & Military Press Ltd
www.nmarchive.com
Published in association with The National Archives

Published by

The Naval & Military Press Ltd

Unit 10 Ridgewood Industrial Park,

Uckfield, East Sussex,

TN22 5QE England

Tel: +44 (0) 1825 749494

www.naval-military-press.com

www.nmarchive.com

This diary has been reprinted in facsimile from the original. Any imperfections are inevitably reproduced and the quality may fall short of modern type and cartographic standards.

© Crown Copyright

Images reproduced by permission of The National Archives, London, England, 2015.

Contents

Document type	Place/Title	Date From	Date To
Heading	WO95/1470/2 526 Field Co Re 1915 Sept-1919 Feb		
Heading	4th Div R.E. 1/1st Durham Field Coy War Diary Sept-Dec, 1915		
Heading	1/1 Fd Co. RE. 18 Sept-Nov Vol. 1		
War Diary	France	18/09/1915	20/09/1915
War Diary	France Mailly Maillet.	21/09/1915	06/10/1915
War Diary	Mailley	07/10/1915	09/10/1915
War Diary	France Mailly Maillet	10/10/1915	12/10/1915
War Diary	Mailly Maillet	13/10/1915	30/10/1915
Miscellaneous	1/1st Division		
War Diary	Mailly	01/12/1915	31/12/1915
Heading	4th Division War Diary 1/1st Durham Field Coy, R.E.S. January To June 1916		
Heading	4th Division I/1st Durham Field Company. Royal Engineers. January 1916		
War Diary	Mailly	01/01/1916	31/01/1916
Heading	4th Division. I/1st Durham Field Company Royal Engineers. February. 1916		
War Diary	Mailly-Maillet	01/02/1916	05/02/1916
War Diary	Mondicourt	06/02/1916	11/02/1916
War Diary	Doullens	12/02/1916	29/02/1916
Heading	4th Division. I/I Durham Field Company. Royal Engineers. March 1916		
War Diary	Doullens	01/03/1916	20/03/1916
War Diary	Bavincourt	21/03/1916	26/03/1916
War Diary	Bienvillers	27/03/1916	31/03/1916
Heading	4th Division. I/1st Durham Field Company. Royal Engineers. April 1916		
War Diary	Bienvillers	01/04/1916	05/04/1916
War Diary	In The Field	06/04/1916	30/04/1916
Heading	4th Division. I/1st Durham Field Company Royal Engineers. May 1916		
War Diary	In The Field	01/05/1916	31/05/1916
War Diary	4th Division. I/1st Durham Field Company. Royal Engineers. June 1916		
War Diary	In The Field.	01/06/1916	30/06/1916
Heading	4th Division War Diary 1/1st Durham Field Coy R.E.S. July, To December 1916		
Heading	4th Division. I/1st Durham Field Company. Royal Engineers. July 1916		
War Diary	Bertrancourt	01/07/1916	01/07/1916
War Diary	In The Field.	01/07/1916	31/07/1916
Heading	4th Division. I/1st Durham Field Company Royal Engineers August 1916		
Miscellaneous	The Officer Commanding, 1/1st Durham Field Coy, R.E. For The Month Of August 1916		
War Diary	Peselhoek Camp. A.20.b.8.8. And Canal Bank.	01/08/1916	20/08/1916
War Diary	Peselhoek Camp A.20.b.8.8	21/08/1916	23/08/1916
War Diary	Post Office Ypres	24/08/1916	24/08/1916
War Diary	Ypres, And Camp H. 13	25/08/1916	31/08/1916

Heading	4th Division. 1/1st Durham Field Company. Royal Engineers. September 1916		
Heading	The Officer Commanding 1/1st Durham Field Coy R.E. For The Month Of September 1916		
War Diary	Post Office. Ypres. & Camp PH.13.c.	01/09/1916	09/09/1916
War Diary	Peselhoek Camp A.15.b.9.5	10/09/1916	17/09/1916
War Diary	Allonville	18/09/1916	24/09/1916
War Diary	Corbie	25/09/1916	25/09/1916
War Diary	Mericourt L' Abbe	26/09/1916	26/09/1916
War Diary	Meaulte	27/09/1916	27/09/1916
War Diary	Carnoy	28/09/1916	30/09/1916
Heading	4th Division. 1/1st Durham Field Company. Royal Engineers. October 1916		
War Diary	Carnoy	01/10/1916	01/10/1916
War Diary	Camp	02/10/1916	02/10/1916
War Diary	F.18.C.5.e.	03/10/1916	09/10/1916
War Diary	Ginchy S.24.b.9.5	10/10/1916	23/10/1916
War Diary	Citadel	24/10/1916	26/10/1916
War Diary	Mericourt	27/10/1916	29/10/1916
War Diary	Allery	30/10/1916	31/10/1916
Heading	4th Division. 1/1st Durham Field Company. Royal Engineers. November 1916		
War Diary	Bouchon	01/11/1916	30/11/1916
Heading	4th Division. 1/1st Durham Field Company. Royal Engineers. December 1916		
War Diary	Bouchon	01/12/1916	02/12/1916
War Diary	Foucaucourt	03/12/1916	08/12/1916
War Diary	Camp 112	09/12/1916	09/12/1916
War Diary	Camp 16	10/12/1916	10/12/1916
War Diary	Camp 16 & Maurepas Ravine	11/12/1916	25/12/1916
War Diary	Camp 16	26/12/1916	31/12/1916
Heading	4th Division. War Diaries 526th Field Coy, R.E. Late 1/1 Durham January, To December 1917 Feb. 1919		
Heading	4 Division. Troops. 406 Field Coy R.E. (Formerely 1/1 Renfrew) 1916 Apr To 1919 June. 526 Field Coy R.E. (Formerely 1/1 Durham) 1915 Sept To 1919 Feb.		
Heading	The Officer Commanding The 1/1st Durham Field Coy. R.E. For January 1917		
War Diary	Sailly-Le-Sec.	01/01/1917	15/01/1917
War Diary	Suzanne	16/01/1917	16/01/1917
War Diary	Curlu.	17/01/1917	22/01/1917
War Diary	Curlu A.29.b.	23/01/1917	23/01/1917
War Diary	Suzanne L.18.a.	24/01/1917	31/01/1917
Heading	The Officer Commanding 526th (Durham) Field Company R.E. (T) For The Month Of February 1917		
War Diary	Suzanne Camp P.c.5. (L.18.a.).	01/02/1917	20/02/1917
War Diary	Camp 117	21/02/1917	21/02/1917
War Diary	Corbie	22/02/1917	28/02/1917
Heading	War Diary By The Officer Commanding 526th (Durham) Field Company. R.E. For The Month Of March 1917		
War Diary	Corbie.	01/03/1917	03/03/1917
War Diary	St. Gratien	04/03/1917	04/03/1917
War Diary	Lavicogne.	05/03/1917	05/03/1917
War Diary	Gezaincourt	06/03/1917	06/03/1917
War Diary	Sericourt	07/03/1917	07/03/1917

War Diary	Savy	08/03/1917	08/03/1917
War Diary	Bray	09/03/1917	31/03/1917
Heading	War Diary By The Officer Commanding 526th (Durham) Field Company R.E. For Month Of April 1917		
War Diary	Bray Near Arras	01/04/1917	10/04/1917
War Diary	H.7.d. Central.	10/04/1917	10/04/1917
War Diary	Fampoux	11/04/1917	11/04/1917
War Diary	H.7.d. Central.	12/04/1917	19/04/1917
War Diary	Larasset	20/04/1917	20/04/1917
War Diary	Izel-Les-Hameau.	21/04/1917	30/04/1917
Heading	War Diary By The Officer Commanding 526th (Durham) Field Coy. R.E. For Month Of May 1917		
War Diary	St. Nicholas	01/05/1917	16/05/1917
War Diary	Arras	17/05/1917	31/05/1917
Heading	War Diary By The Officer Commanding 526th (Durham) Field Co. R.E. For Month Of June 1917		
War Diary	Tilloy-Les-Hermaville.	01/06/1917	10/06/1917
War Diary	Arras	11/06/1917	11/06/1917
War Diary	Blangy.	12/06/1917	30/06/1917
Heading	War Diary By The Officer Commanding 526th (Durham) Field Co. R.E. for July 1917		
War Diary	Blangy. (H.19.c.5.8.)	01/07/1917	31/07/1917
Heading	War Diary By The Officer Commanding 526th (Durham) Field Coy R.E. For Month Of August 1917		
War Diary	Blangy (H.19.c.5.8.)	01/08/1917	31/08/1917
Heading	War Diary Of The Officer Commanding 526th (Durham) Field Co. R.E. From 1st September To 30th September 1917		
War Diary	Blangy. H.19.c.5.8	01/09/1917	04/09/1917
War Diary	Ransart.	05/09/1917	21/09/1917
War Diary	Putlows Camps F.10.a.5.2	22/09/1917	28/09/1917
War Diary	B.23.h.6.4	29/09/1917	30/09/1917
Heading	War Diary of The Officer Commanding, 526th (Durham) Field Co. R.E. From 1st October To 31st October. 1917		
War Diary	Ref. Sheet Belgium 28.N.W. B.23.b.6.4	01/10/1917	04/10/1917
War Diary	B.23.b.6.4	04/10/1917	12/10/1917
War Diary	Portland Camp X.28.a	13/10/1917	15/10/1917
War Diary	Poperinghe	16/10/1917	18/10/1917
War Diary	Wanquetin	19/10/1917	22/10/1917
War Diary	N.2.d.5.7	23/10/1917	31/10/1917
Heading	War Diary of The Officer Commanding, 526th (Durham) Field Co. R.E. From 1st November To 30th November 1917		
War Diary	N.2.d.5.7. (Sheet:- 51.)	01/11/1917	09/11/1917
War Diary	N.2.d.5.7	10/11/1917	30/11/1917
Heading	War Diary Of The Officer Commanding, 526th (Durham) Field Co R.E. From 1st December To 31st December 1917		
War Diary	N.2.d.5.7. (Ref Sheet 51.b.S.W.)	01/12/1917	02/12/1917
War Diary	Happy Valley (H.36.a.10.15) Ref Sheet 51.B.N.W.	03/12/1917	31/12/1917
Heading	4th Division. 526th Field Company R.E. January, To December 1918 Jan-Feb. 1919		

Heading	War Diary Of The Officer Commanding 526th (Durham) Field Co. R.E. From 1st January To 31st January 1918		
War Diary	Happy Valley H.36.a.10.05. Ref Sheet 51.B.N.W.	01/01/1918	04/02/1918
War Diary	Schramm Barracks Arras	05/02/1918	15/02/1918
War Diary	Arras	16/02/1918	28/02/1918
Heading	4th Div. 526th (Durham) Field Company, R.E. March 1918		
Heading	War Diary of The Officer Commanding 526th (Durham) Field Co. R.E. From 1st March To 31st March 1918		
War Diary	Arras	01/03/1918	21/03/1918
War Diary	Stirling Camp H.13.d.7.8	22/03/1918	22/03/1918
War Diary	Etrun.	23/03/1918	28/03/1918
War Diary	Stirling Camp H.13.d.7.8	29/03/1918	31/03/1918
Heading	4th Divisional Engineers 526th (Durham) Field Company R.E. April 1918		
Heading	War Diary of The Officer Commanding 526th (Durham) Of Field Company R.E. From 1st April To 30th April 1918		
War Diary	Stirling Camp H.13.b.9.25. (Sheet 51.B. N.W.)	01/04/1918	02/04/1918
War Diary	St. Laurent Blangy G.18.e.5.4	03/04/1918	07/04/1918
War Diary	'Y' Hutments L.1.a.9.5. (Sheet 51c NE)	08/04/1918	09/04/1918
War Diary	Haute Avesnes	10/04/1918	11/04/1918
War Diary	Le Hamel	12/04/1918	13/04/1918
War Diary	Chateau De Werppe W.19.a.7.2	14/04/1918	27/04/1918
War Diary	V.23.a.0.9. (near-Lenglet)	28/04/1918	30/04/1918
Heading	War Diary of The Officer Commanding 526th (Durham) Field Company R.E. From 1st May To 31st May 1918		
War Diary	Sheet 36 A. V.23.A.0.9	01/05/1918	13/05/1918
War Diary	Busnettes	14/05/1918	31/05/1918
Heading	War Diary of The Officer Commanding 526th (Durham) Field Company R.E. From 1st June To 30th June 1918		
War Diary	Busnettes	01/06/1918	30/06/1918
Heading	War Diary of The Officer Commanding 526th (Durham) Field Company R.E. From 1st July To 31st July 1918		
War Diary	Busnettes	01/07/1918	31/07/1918
Heading	War Diary of The Officer Commanding 526th (Durham) Field Company R.E. From 1st August To 31st August 1918		
War Diary	Busnettes.	01/08/1918	18/08/1918
War Diary	Gonnehem	19/08/1918	22/08/1918
War Diary	Busnettes.	23/08/1918	23/08/1918
War Diary	Rely.	24/08/1918	24/08/1918
War Diary	Ternas	25/08/1918	25/08/1918
War Diary	Bouvigny.	26/08/1918	26/08/1918
War Diary	Bois-de-Bouvigny.	27/08/1918	27/08/1918
War Diary	Happy-Valley.	28/08/1918	31/08/1918
Heading	War Diary of The Officer Commanding 526th (Durham) Field Company R.E. From 1st September To 30th September 1918		
War Diary	French Near Bois du Very.	01/09/1918	01/09/1918
War Diary	Remy.	02/09/1918	03/09/1918

War Diary	Mingoval	04/09/1918	18/09/1918
War Diary	Monchy () Sheet 51B. D.7.a.0.8	19/09/1918	30/09/1918
Miscellaneous	War Diary-AC 406th (Renfrew). Field Coy. R.E.		
Heading	War Diary of The Officer Commanding 526th (Durham) Field Company R.E. From 1st October To 31st October 1918		
War Diary	Monchy (Vicinity) Sheet 51.B.0.7.a.0.8	01/10/1918	06/10/1918
War Diary	Dainville.	07/10/1918	10/10/1918
War Diary	Boulon Wood (Vicinity)	11/10/1918	12/10/1918
War Diary	Escaudoeuvres	13/10/1918	17/10/1918
War Diary	Naves.	18/10/1918	20/10/1918
War Diary	Avesnes-Le-Sec.	21/10/1918	23/10/1918
War Diary	Haspres.	24/10/1918	31/10/1918
Heading	War Diary of The Officer Commanding, 526th (Durham) Field Company R.E. From 1st November To 30th November. 1918		
War Diary	Haspres.	01/11/1918	03/11/1918
War Diary	Maing	04/11/1918	08/11/1918
War Diary	Sebourg	09/11/1918	09/11/1918
War Diary	Audregnies. (Belgium)	10/11/1918	11/11/1918
War Diary	Audregnies	12/11/1918	18/11/1918
War Diary	Curgies. (France)	19/11/1918	19/11/1918
War Diary	Saultain	20/11/1918	30/11/1918
War Diary	War Diary of The Officer Commanding 526th (Durham) Field Company R.E. From 1st December To 31st December 1918		
War Diary	Saultain.	01/12/1918	31/12/1918
Heading	War Diary of The Officer Commanding, 526th (Durham) Field Coy. R.E. From 1st January To 31st January, 1919		
War Diary	Saultain.	01/01/1919	05/01/1919
War Diary	Morlanwelz (Belgium)	05/01/1919	15/01/1919
War Diary	Morlanwelz	16/01/1919	31/01/1919
Heading	War Diary of The Officer Commanding 526th (Durham) Field Coy. R.E. From. February 1st To February 28th-1919		
War Diary	Morlanwelz	01/02/1919	28/02/1919

WO 95 1470/2

526 FIELD CO RE

1915 SEPT - 1919 FEB

Index	SUBJECT.	

(526 Fld Coy RE) 4TH DIV

No.	Contents.	Date.

R.E.

1/1st DURHAM FIELD COY.

WAR DIARY
SEPT.- DEC., 1915

4th Division

1/1 Dunham 2d Co. M.E.

18 Sep 81 — Nov

Vol I.

121/7718

Army Form C. 2118

WAR DIARY
or
INTELLIGENCE SUMMARY

(Erase heading not required.)

1/1st. DURHAM FIELD COMPANY R.E.

Instructions regarding War Diaries and Intelligence Summaries are contained in F. S. Regs., Part II. and the Staff Manual respectively. Title pages will be prepared in manuscript.

Hour, Date, Place	Summary of Events and Information	Remarks and references to Appendices
FRANCE Sept 18th 1915		
5 am	Arrived at HAVRE	
7 am	Disembarked	
2 pm	Left HAVRE for rest camp	
4 pm	Arrived at Rest camp.	
Sept 19. 4 am	Left rest camp to entrain	
10 pm	Arrived at DOULLENS and marched to AUTHIEULLE	
Sept 20: 2 am	Arrived at AUTHIEULLE	
8 am	Marched from AUTHIEULLE to MAILLY-MAILLET.	
4 pm	Arrived at MAILLY-MAILLET.	
7.4 pm	Lieut WEIR & party went round 2nd line trenches at VITERMONT with Lieut BRETHERTON of WEST LANCASHIRE FIELD Co R.E.	

O.C. 1/1st. Durham Field Coy. R.E.
[signature] Major.

Army Form C. 2118

WAR DIARY
or
INTELLIGENCE SUMMARY
(Erase heading not required.)

1/1st. DURHAM FIELD COMPANY R.E.

Instructions regarding War Diaries and Intelligence Summaries are contained in F.S. Regs., Part II. and the Staff Manual respectively. Title Pages will be prepared in manuscript.

Place	Date	Hour	Summary of Events and Information	Remarks and references to Appendices
FRANCE	Sept 21st 1915	9 am	Parties employed on front line trenches at SHEFIELD, well at Tuesday R².	
MAILLY			No 3 Section attached to rear line Tuesday R² for both.	
MAILLET	22nd		No 4 Section on detachment duty at MESNIL, carrying at " " Section and reporting to LIEUT. THORNE of rear line R².	
		7.30 pm.	Sections employed on trenches &c day & night parties.	
	23rd		Sapper ECCLES wounded in the head by shrapnel whilst working on wire entanglement between VITERMONT–MAILLEY. Sections working on 3rd Line defences trenches, on keep wire entanglements. Village shelled today, one killed was struck.	
	24th		Sections employed on works day & night work.	
	25th		Sections employed on works day & night work. Machine gun emplacements	

Amsbury Major.
O.C. 1/1st. Durham Field Company R.E.

1875. W. W593/826 1,000,000 4/15 J.B.C. & A. A.D.S.S./Forms/C. 2118.

O.C. 1/1st. Durham Field Company R.E. Major.

Army Form C. 2118

WAR DIARY
or
INTELLIGENCE SUMMARY
(*Erase heading not required.*)

1/1st. DURHAM FIELD COMPANY R.E.

Instructions regarding War Diaries and Intelligence Summaries are contained in F. S. Regs., Part II. and the Staff Manual respectively. Title Pages will be prepared in manuscript.

Place	Date	Hour	Summary of Events and Information	Remarks and references to Appendices
FRANCE	1915 Sept			
MAILLY	26th		Nos 1 & 3 Sections on trenches & Gun emplacements; Dugouts No 4 working on Dugouts on MESNIL – MARTINSART road.	
MAILLET	27th		Same as 26th – No 2 Section now detached from best Lane Jealans R.E. Aeroplane dropped bombs on village 5.30 p.m.	
	28th		Sections working on trenches, Gun emplacements & dug outs day & night work. No 1 Section completed dugout on MESNIL – MARTINSART road.	
	29th		Sections employed on dugouts machine gun emplacements, No 1 Section 2nd line defences at Brigade Headquarts. MARTINSART.	
	30-		General Inspection of Sections Equipment Etc.	

AmDerry Major.
O.C. 1/1st. Durham Field Coy. R.E.

Major.

Army Form C.2118

WAR DIARY
or
INTELLIGENCE SUMMARY   1/1st. DURHAM FIELD COMPANY R.E.

(Erase heading not required.)

Instructions regarding War Diaries and Intelligence Summaries are contained in F.S. Regs., Part II. and the Staff Manual respectively. Title Pages will be prepared in manuscript.

Place	Date	Hour	Summary of Events and Information	Remarks and references to Appendices
FRANCE	1915 Oct 1st		No 1 Section on 2nd line trenches. Gun emplacements and trenches with infantry party. No 2 Section laying trench boards. Work done by No 4 Section at No 3 Redan. Work over No 3 Redan at AUCHNVILLERS.	
MAILLY			MESNIL, and No 4 took over No 3 work at AUCHONVILLERS.	
MAILLET	2nd		No 1 Section on trenches and infantry party, and gun emplacements. No 2 Section with No 3 Section of 9th Fusiliers R.E. under LIEUT. HOMER. No 3 Section attached to West Lancs Field Coy R.E. reporting to LIEUT. THORNE. Commenced work on trenches at Anzonl. No 4 on trenches at AUCHONVILLERS, and village defences.	

Amsett. Major.
O.C. 1/1st. Durham Field Coy. R.E.

Army Form C. 2118

WAR DIARY
or
INTELLIGENCE SUMMARY
(Erase heading not required.)

1/1st. DURHAM FIELD COMPANY R.E.

Instructions regarding War Diaries and Intelligence Summaries are contained in F.S. Regs., Part II. and the Staff Manual respectively. Title Pages will be prepared in manuscript.

Place	Date 1915	Hour	Summary of Events and Information	Remarks and references to Appendices
FRANCE	Oct 3rd		No 1 Section on gun emplacements & communication trenches with infantry party	
MAILLY			No 2 Section same as Oct 2nd	
MAILLET			No 3 Section employed on dug outs & routing trenches with infantry at MESNIL.	
			No 4 Section trenches & village defences at ACHONVILLERS	
	4.		Same as states for Oct 3rd	
	5.		Same as states for Oct 3rd	
	6.		Nos 1, 2 & 3. Same as stated for Oct 3rd.	
			No 4 making screen for HAMEL road to protect from snipers, night work in trenches with party of infantry.	

A.W.Perry Major.
O.G. 1/1st. Durham Field Coy. R.E.

1875 Wt. W593/826 1,000,000 4/15 J.B.C. & A. A.D.S.S./Forms/C. 2118.

WAR DIARY
INTELLIGENCE SUMMARY

(Erase heading not required.)

Army Form C. 2118

1/1st. DURHAM FIELD COMPANY R.E.

Place	Date	Hour	Summary of Events and Information	Remarks and references to Appendices
MAILLY-MAILLET	6.		No 1 Section General inspection of equipment etc	
	7.		" 2 " " " "	
			" 3 " repairing trenches & defence of village at ACHONVILLERS.	
			" 4 " dugouts or MESNIL	
	8.		" 1 " widening & deepening trenches and for laying pipes	
			" 2 " Employed on trenches any work & laying pipes	
			for water supply	
			No 3 & 4 Sections same as Oct 7.	
	9.		No 1 Section fire communication trenches FORT ANLEY	
			with infantry parties.	
			No 2 Section trucking out and making ump covers	
			ACHONVILLERS.	
			No 3 Section Communication trenches and for MESNIL	
			with infantry parties	
			No 4 Section same as Oct 8.	

AWDerry
Major.
O.C. 1/1st. Durham Field Coy. R.E.

Army Form C. 2118

WAR DIARY
or
INTELLIGENCE SUMMARY
(Erase heading not required.)

1/1st. DURHAM FIELD COMPANY R.E.

Instructions regarding War Diaries and Intelligence Summaries are contained in F.S. Regs., Part II. and the Staff Manual respectively. Title Pages will be prepared in manuscript.

Place	Date	Hour	Summary of Events and Information	Remarks and references to Appendices
FRANCE	Oct 1/15 10-		No 1 Section with infantry party on communication trench from FORT ANLEY.	
MAILLY			No 2 Section repairing trenches, making dump at AUCHONVILLERS	
MAILLET			No 4 Section Revetting & repairing parados & traverses & cutting Communication trenches at AV. S.	
			No 3 Section left MESNIL at 2.30 pm for MAILLY.	
	11th		Nos 1 & 4 Sections came as Oct 10th	
			No 2. Trenches at AUCHONVILLERS & communication trench MESNIL ROAD	
			No 3 Sec Cutting trenches at AUCHONVILLERS held	
			Party of infantry night work.	
	12th "		No 1 Section on tunnel under VITERMONT ROAD. day & night work.	
			" 2 " Communication trench FORT ANLEY	
			" 3 " Same as Oct 11th	
			" 4 " Same as Oct 11th and dugouts at TENDERLOIN.	

Cam. Sent Major.
O.C. 1/1st. Durham Field Coy. R.E.

Army Form C. 2118

WAR DIARY
or
INTELLIGENCE SUMMARY
(Erase heading not required.)

1/1st. DURHAM FIELD COMPANY R.E.

Place	Date 1915	Hour	Summary of Events and Information	Remarks and references to Appendices
MAILLY MAILLET	Oct 13th		Sections employed same as 12th October.	
	14th		" do " " " " " "	
	15th		" " " " 13th October	
			No 1 Section on dugouts at TENDERLOIN, and tunnel under VITERMONT road.	
			No 2 Section Communication Trench FORT ANLEY.	
			No 3 Section Same as Oct 13th	
			No 4 " " " Oct 13th	
	16th		No 1 " Dugouts Communication Trenches AV 23.	
			" 2 " Same as Oct 15th	
			" 3 " " " 15th "	
			" 4 " Improving & Revetting A.W.10 A.V.22 & A.V.23	

[signature]
Major.
O.C. 1/1st. Durham Field Coy. R.E.

Army Form C. 2118

WAR DIARY
or
INTELLIGENCE SUMMARY   1/1st. DURHAM FIELD COMPANY R.E.

(Erase heading not required.)

Instructions regarding War Diaries and Intelligence Summaries are contained in F.S. Regs., Part II. and the Staff Manual respectively. Title Pages will be prepared in manuscript.

Place	Date 1915	Hour	Summary of Events and Information	Remarks and references to Appendices
MAILLY	Oct 17th		No 1 Section on Dugouts at TENDERLAIN & relaying trench boards in 2nd Avenue. Day & night work.	
			No 2. Section Communication trench FORT ANLEY.	
			No 3 Section improving trenches, & making hurdles for camps	AV 22 & 23
			No 4 Cutting Communication trenches rear of	AV 22 & 23.
	18-		No 1 Section same as 17th October.	
			" 2 " " 17th -"-	
			" 3 " improving trenches with infantry party	
			" 4 " Improving fire trenches	AV 19. 22. & 23.
	19-		No 1 " Same as Oct 17th	
			" 2 " -"- -"- 17th	
			" 3 " Same as Octr 18th	
			" 4 " " " 18th Communication trench rear of AV 23.	

A. W. Doherty Major.
O.C. 1/1st. Durham Field Coy R.E.

WAR DIARY or INTELLIGENCE SUMMARY

Army Form C. 2118

1/1st. DURHAM FIELD COMPANY R.E.

Place	Date 1915	Hour	Summary of Events and Information	Remarks and references to Appendices
MAILLY MAILLET	Oct 20th		No 1. Section. dugouts at TENDERLOIN, & revetting recess in ESSEX St. day work	
			No 2 Section trenches at AUCHONVILLERS, and communication trench FORTANLEY & A.V.5.	
			No 3 Section. Same as October 19th	
	21st		" 4 " — Repair of fire trenches Artillery communication trench. Construction of dugout in rear of A.V. 23.	
			No 1 Section Same as Oct 20 — & inspection.	
			No 2 Section Inspection of equipment etc etc	
			3 " Inspection of equipment etc	
			4 " — " — " —	
	22nd		No 1 Section dugouts, revetting trenches. Listening post will. Infantry party, work interrupted owing to infantry party having to "stand to"	
			No 2 Section. Improving trenches AUCHONVILLERS.	
			No 3 " Improving trenches AUCHONVILLERS.	
			" 4 " Repairing & thickening of hedge AUCHONVILLERS.	

O.C. 1/1st. Durham Field Coy R.E.
Major.

Army Form C. 2118.

WAR DIARY
or
INTELLIGENCE SUMMARY
(Erase heading not required.)

Instructions regarding War Diaries and Intelligence Summaries are contained in F. S. Regs., Part II. and the Staff Manual respectively. Title pages will be prepared in manuscript.

1/1st. DURHAM FIELD COMPANY R.E.

Hour, Date, Place	Summary of Events and Information	Remarks and references to Appendices
1915		
MAILLY-MAILLET	No. 1 Section same as Oct. 22nd 1915.	
Oct. 23rd		
" 2 "	" " " " 22nd " 1915.	
" 3 "	" " Trenches with infantry say Mughabirotta	
" 4 "	" " Continuation of Communication trench rear of A V 22 & 23. repairing construction of rev trench. also dug out hedge thickening.	
Oct. 24th	No. 1 Section same as Oct. 22nd	
" 2 "	" " Draining trenches	
" 3 "	" " New trench AUCHON & MESNIL road improving trench at AUCHON. Apr trench PORT ANLEY	
" 4 "	" " Same as Oct. 23rd.	
Oct. 25th	No. 1 " Same as Oct. 23rd.	
" 2 "	" " Oct. 23rd.	
" 3 "	" " Inspection of Equipment etc	
" 4 "	" " - do -	

O.C. 1/1st. Durham Field Coy. R.E. Major.

WAR DIARY
or
INTELLIGENCE SUMMARY

(Erase heading not required.)

Army Form C. 2118.

1/1st. DURHAM FIELD COMPANY R.E.

Hour, Date, Place	Summary of Events and Information	Remarks and references to Appendices
MAILLY-MAILLET 1915		
Oct. 26th	No.1 Section same as Oct. 23rd	
2	" draining trenches opp. trench ANICHON and FORT ANLEY.	
3	" Same as Oct. 24th	
4	" Repairing fire trenches dugouts at A.Vs. 1 to 7. 10, 22 & 23	
Oct. 27th	No.1 Section same as Oct. 23rd	
2	" communication trench FORT ANLEY	
3	" draining FORT ANLEY trench	
4	" Screening, fire stepping & repair of fire trench in general. A.Vs. 4, 6, 7, 22 & 23.	
Oct. 28th	No.1 Section same as Oct. 23rd	
2	" draining communication trench FORT ANLEY.	
3	" repairing dug outs FORTRESS ROAD.	
4	" Repairing trenches A.Vs # 6,7,10 22 & 23.	

O.C. 1/1st. Durham Field Coy. R.E.

Major.

Army Form C. 2118.

WAR DIARY
or
INTELLIGENCE SUMMARY
(Erase heading not required.)

1/1st. DURHAM FIELD COMPANY R.E.

Hour, Date, Place	Summary of Events and Information	Remarks and references to Appendices
MAILLY-MAILLET Oct 29th	No 1 Section Dugouts at TENDERLOIN & front line trenches	
	No 2 Section communication [trench?] [reserve?] FORT ANLEY.	
	No 3 S. Fixed information for observation post in AUCHONVILLERS. Improving French Auction. [making?] handles for drains.	
Oct 30	No 1 Section Same as Oct 29th	
	No 2 " Same as Oct 29th	
	No 3 " Observation Post. Trenches with Infantry Party AUCHON, [breastwork?] and drain FORTRESS ROAD.	
31st	No 1 " Same as Oct 29th	
	No 1 Section Dugouts rest trench 60 & CARDIFF	
	2 " Inspection of equipment.	
	3 " Inspection of equipment. EG	
	— " —	

[signature]
O.C. 1/1st. Durham Field Co.R.E.
Major.

Army Form C. 2118.

WAR DIARY
or
INTELLIGENCE SUMMARY   1/1st. DURHAM FIELD COMPANY R.E.

(Erase heading not required.)

Hour, Date, Place	Summary of Events and Information	Remarks and references to Appendices
MAILLY-MAILLET. November 1st	No1 Section Dugouts at TENDERLOIN for Infantry trenches, with infantry parties day and night work.	
	No 2 Section trenches at FORTANLEY & touching Wilken trenches at FORCEVILLE.	
	No 3 Section Observation Post at AUCHON & trenches leading to FORT ANLEY.	
	No 4 Section. Construction of Dugouts AV22 & trenches AV5. 22. 7. 6. 4. and repair of gun trenches. Infantry parties.	
November 2nd	No1 Section Same as Nov 1st	
	2 " Same as Nov 1st	
	3 " Same as Nov 1st	
	4 " Same as Nov 1st	

Ann Derry Major.
O.C. 1/1st. Durham Field Company R.E.

Army Form C. 2118.

WAR DIARY
or
INTELLIGENCE SUMMARY

1/1st. DURHAM FIELD COMPANY R.E.

(Erase heading not required.)

Hour, Date, Place	Summary of Events and Information	Remarks and references to Appendices
MAILLY-MAILLET November 3rd	No 1. Section Front Line trenches TENDERLOIN REDAN & CHATHAM. No 2 Section cleaning Communication trench FORT ANLEY. No 3 Section Observation post trenches at ATACHON & FORT ANLEY. No 4 Section Construction of machine gun emplacements AV 23. Dugouts AV 22. Repairing firetrenches A.V. 4 & S 6 & 22.	
November 4	Same as November 3rd for all sections.	

A M Derry
Major.
O.C. 1/1st. Durham Field Company R.E.

Army Form C. 2118.

WAR DIARY
or
INTELLIGENCE SUMMARY

(Erase heading not required.)

1/1st. DURHAM FIELD COMPANY R.E.

Hour, Date, Place	Summary of Events and Information	Remarks and references to Appendices

MAILLY-MAILLET No 1 Section dugouts from the line trenches
November 5th   at TENDERLOIN & REDAN
              No 2 Section trenches FORTANKEY?
              building Athletes trenches at ACHEUX arm

              FORCEVILLE.
              No 3 Section Observation post at AUCHON
              trenches on FORTRESS ROAD.

              No 4 Section. Cutter on trench work in
              front line with infantry parties

November 6th No 1 Section same as November 5th.
              " 2   "   "   "   "   "
              " 3   "   "   "   "   "
              " 4   "   "   "   "   "

A M Dearly Major.
O.C. 1/1st. Durham Field Company R.E.

Army Form C. 2118.

WAR DIARY
or
INTELLIGENCE SUMMARY
(Erase heading not required.)

1/1st. DURHAM FIELD COMPANY R.E.

Instructions regarding War Diaries and Intelligence Summaries are contained in F.S. Regs, Part II. and the Staff Manual respectively. Title pages will be prepared in manuscript.

Hour, Date, Place	Summary of Events and Information	Remarks and references to Appendices
MAILLY-MAILLET November 7-	No 1 Section from Run trenches dug outs at TENDERLOIN & REDAN " 2 -" " Fire trench. Communication trench at FORT ANLEY, ablution trenches & sheds at ACHEUX & FORCEVILLE. No 3 Section Observation post AUCHON. Heavily shelled today, one caught by shell knocked over observation post, one man 2 Off. & one wounded in back by shell splinter. worker trenches front of AUCHON. No 4 Section same as No 6 - " 1 Section " Fire trenches day & night work.	
November 8 -	No 2 Section. General Inspection and erection of Ablution sheds at ACHEUX & FORCEVILLE No 3 Section General inspection of dugouts on 6/L " 4 -"- Same as November 6 -	

Ann Perry Major.
O.C. 1/1st. Durham Field Company R.E.

Army Form C. 2118.

WAR DIARY
or
INTELLIGENCE SUMMARY

(Erase heading not required.)

1/1st. DURHAM FIELD COMPANY R.E.

Instructions regarding War Diaries and Intelligence Summaries are contained in F. S. Regs., Part II. and the Staff Manual respectively. Title pages will be prepared in manuscript.

Hour, Date, Place	Summary of Events and Information	Remarks and references to Appendices
MAILLY - MAILLET.		
November 9th	No 1 Section same as Nov 8th.	
	" 2 " drawing trenches FORT ANLEY.	
	" 3 " Observation Post & trenches AUCHON	
	and addition trenches at ACHEUX.	
November 10th	" 4 " Same as Nov 8th	
	No 1 Section same as Nov 8th	
	" 2 " " " " 9th	
	" 3 " " " " 9th	
	" 4 " " " " 6th and A.V. 23.	
	machine gun emplacement TENDERLOIN reform	
November 11th	No 1 Section employed on erection of ablution	
	line trenches	
	No 2 Section employed on erection of ablution	
	trenches sheds at ACHEUX & FORCEVILLE.	
	No 3 Section same as November 10th	
	" 4 " " " " 10th	
	Capt Cutt proceeded to England to take up	
	commission in the infantry.	

O.C. 1/1st. Durham Field Company R.E.

A.W. Derry Major.

Army Form C. 2118.

WAR DIARY
or
INTELLIGENCE SUMMARY

1/1st. DURHAM FIELD COMPANY R.E.

(Erase heading not required.)

Hour, Date, Place	Summary of Events and Information	Remarks and references to Appendices
MAILLEY MAILLET. November 12th	No 1 Section took up trenches dug out as TENDERLOIN REDAN. No 2 Section supervising the erection of Wilson trenches, huts at ACHEUX & FORCEVILLE. No 3 Section Clearmaker poor + trenches at AUCHON. No 4 Section Same as November 11th.	
November 13th	All sections employed at duties for November 12th.	
November 14th	All sections employed as stated for November 12th.	
November 15th	All Sections employed as stated for November 12th.	Ann Jerry O.C. 1/1st. Durham Field Coy. R.E.

WAR DIARY
or
INTELLIGENCE SUMMARY

(Erase heading not required.)

Army Form C. 2118.

1/1st. DURHAM FIELD COMPANY R.E.

Hour, Date, Place	Summary of Events and Information	Remarks and references to Appendices
MAILLEY MAILLET. November 16th	No 1 Section employed on front line trenches by night. With 2nd infantry parties at TENDERLOIN REDAN, & aboution No 2 Section supervising trellising of trenches and dug outs at ACHEUX & FORCEVILLE No 3 Section obtaining post trenches at ARCH ON 2nd infantry parties No 4 Section employed same as No 1 Section.	
November 17th	No 1 & 4 Sections employed on details for Nov 16th 2 Section same as stated for Nov 16th 3 Sam as stated for Nov 16th	
November 18th	No 1 & 4 Section same as stated for Nov 16th 2 Section same as Nov 16th 3 Sam as Nov 16th & Revetting ANLEY	

AM Leary
Major.
O.C. 1/1st. Durham Field Coy. R.E.

Army Form C. 2118.

WAR DIARY
or
INTELLIGENCE SUMMARY

1/1st. DURHAM FIELD COMPANY R.E.

(Erase heading not required.)

Instructions regarding War Diaries and Intelligence Summaries are contained in F. S. Regs., Part II. and the Staff Manual respectively. Title pages will be prepared in manuscript.

Hour, Date, Place	Summary of Events and Information	Remarks and references to Appendices
MAILLEY-MAILLET. November 19th	No 1 & 4 Sections on front line trenches at TENDERLOIN, CHATHAM & CARDIFF. No 2 Section supervising the erection of abrison trenches, and ↓ at ACHEUX and FORCEVILLE. No 3 Section Observation post erecting hut ANLEY.	
November 20th	No 1 & 4 Sections same as Nov 19th. No 2 Section " " " 19th - No 3 " " " " 19 -	
November 21st	No 1, 3 & 4 Sections General inspection of equipment etc. No 2 Section same as Nov 19th -	

O.C. 1/1st. Durham Field Co.R.E.

Army Form C. 2118.

WAR DIARY
or
INTELLIGENCE SUMMARY

1/1st. DURHAM FIELD COMPANY R.E.

(Erase heading not required.)

Hour, Date, Place	Summary of Events and Information	Remarks and references to Appendices
MAILLEY MAILLET. November 22nd 1915.	No 1 & 4 Sections on front line trenches at TENDERLOIN, CHATHAM, & CARDIFF. No 2 Section supervising feeding of Alluvion trenches & huts at AUCHEUX & FORCEVILLE. No 3 Section observation post AUCHON & working trenches at ANLEY.	
November 23rd	All sections employed same as Nov 22nd	
November 24th	Nos 1 & 4 nd same as Nov 22nd Section. No 3 Section observation post AUCHON drawing ANLEY trench, improving VILLERS trench, wire entanglement.	
November 25th & 26th	All sections employed same as Nov 24th. Sapper C F Harry proceeded to England to be transferred to Engineers Reserve as an Engineer Cadet Officer.	A.M. Denny Major O.C. 1/1st. Durham Field Co. R.E.

Army Form C. 2118.

WAR DIARY
or
INTELLIGENCE SUMMARY

1/1st. DURHAM FIELD COMPANY R.E.

(Erase heading not required.)

Hour, Date, Place	Summary of Events and Information	Remarks and references to Appendices
MAILLY-MAILLET November 26th	All sections employed same as Nov 25th	
" 27th	Nos 1, 3 + 4 general inspection of Equipment &c No 2 Section employed same as Nov 25th	
" 28th	No 1st Section on front line trenches at REDAN, CARDIFF, CHATHM, TENDERLOIN No 2 Section same as Nov 25th " 3 " — Observation post trenches AUCHON " 4 " Wire entanglement VILLERS trench	
" 29th	Nos 1st Sections same as Nov 28th " 2 Section same as 25th " 3 " " 28th " 4 " " 28th	
30.	Nos 1 + 4 Sections same as 28th " 2 Section " " 25th " 3 " drawing improving trenches AUCHON wire entanglement VILLERS trench	

A M Scott
O.C. 1/1st. Durham Field Coy. R.E.

1/32 Dunham 2.C.R.C.

See
vol II

4th Div

Army Form C. 2118

WAR DIARY
or
INTELLIGENCE SUMMARY
(Erase heading not required.)

1/1st Durham Field Coy. R.E.

Place	Date	Hour	Summary of Events and Information	Remarks and references to Appendices
MAILLY	Dec 1st		Nos 1 & 4 Sections on front line trenches in REDAN CHATHAM & CARDIFF. Dugouts at TENDERLOIN. Both parties of infantry day & night work.	
			No 2 Section superintending the erection of Ablution trenches & latrines, drying sheds at AUCHEUX & FORCEVILLE.	
			No 3 Section improving draining trenches etc. and wire entanglements at AUCHONVILLERS, with party of infantry day & night work.	
	2nd		All Sections working same as Dec 1st.	
	3rd		Nos 1, 2, 4 same as Dec 1st. No 3 Section inspection of equipment Etc.	
	4th		Nos 1, 2, 4 same as Dec 3rd. No 3 Section draining and revetting wire entanglement at AUCHONVILLERS.	

for O/C 1/1st Durham Field Coy. R.E.
J.B. Wakeman
Major

Army Form C. 2118

WAR DIARY
or
INTELLIGENCE SUMMARY
(Erase heading not required.)

1/1st DURHAM FIELD CO. R.E.

Place	Date	Hour	Summary of Events and Information	Remarks and references to Appendices
MAILLY	Dec 4th		Same for Rections as last.	
	5th		do	
	6th		do	
	7th		do	
	8th		No 1.3 at Rections Inspector of Arms & Equipment etc. No 2 Section same as stated for last.	
	9th		No 1 at Rections from fire trenches REDAN CHATHAM CARDIFF & 3rd Avenue. New trench ROMAN ROAD, Hub. Sapout at TEN DERLOIN. No 2 Section same as last. No 3 " Revetting trenches at AUCHONVILLERS, & wire entanglements.	
	10th		All Rections same as last.	

for O/C J.R. Melmajor

1/1st DURHAM FIELD CO. R.E.

1875 Wt. W593/826 1,000,000 4/15 J.B.C. & A. A.D.S.S./Forms/C. 2118.

WAR DIARY
or
INTELLIGENCE SUMMARY
(Erase heading not required.)

Army Form C. 2118

Place	Date	Hour	Summary of Events and Information	Remarks and references to Appendices
MAILLY.	Dec 11th		Sections employed as stated on Dec 10th	
	12th		do	
	13th	7 hrs	1, 3 & 4 Sections inspection of arms & equipment	
			No 2 Section as stated for Dec 10th	
	14th	7.00	1 & 4 Sections front line trenches REDAN – CHATHAM CARDIFF & 3rd AVENUE. Dugouts TENDERLOIN. No 2 Section supervising erection of Aubusson trenches. Latrines, Drying sheds at ACHEUX & FORCEVILLE. No 3 Section revetting ANLEY trench & avenues 4-5-6-7 Spare entanglement at VILLERS trench	
	15th		All Sections as for 14th	

Army Form C. 2118

WAR DIARY
or
INTELLIGENCE SUMMARY
(Erase heading not required.)

Place	Date	Hour	Summary of Events and Information	Remarks and references to Appendices
MAILLY	1915 Dec 16th		No 1 & 4 Sections on front line trenches at REDAN, CHATHAM, CARDIFF, & 3rd AVENUE. Dugouts TEN DER WIN. No 2 Section supervising erection of Ablution benches & drying sheds, at ACHEUX & FORCEVILLE. No 3 Section Communication trench we we encampment AVELUY & ANCHONVILLERS.	
	17th		All sections same as Dec 16th	
	18th		Nos 1. 3 & 4 Sections inspection of Arms & Equipment Etc. No 2 Section same as 16th Dec.	16th
	19th		All sections same as 16th	16th
	20th		do	16th
	21st		do	16th
	and 22		do	16th

for O.C. [signature] Major
1/1st [illegible]

Army Form C. 2118

WAR DIARY
or
INTELLIGENCE SUMMARY

(Erase heading not required.)

1/1ST DURHAM FIELD CO. R.E.

Instructions regarding War Diaries and Intelligence Summaries are contained in F. S. Regs., Part II. and the Staff Manual respectively. Title Pages will be prepared in manuscript.

Place	Date	Hour	Summary of Events and Information	Remarks and references to Appendices
MAILLY	Dec 23rd		All sections employed as per Dec 16th scale	
	24th		do	
	25th		Xmas day. Inspection of equipment etc.	
	26th		No 1 Section on front line trenches at REDAN, CHATHAM + CARDIFF. Dugouts at TENDERLOIN. Day & night work with infantry parties.	
			No 2 Section supervising erection of abattis trenches, latrines + drying shelters at ACHEUX + FORCEVILLE.	
			" 3 Section Revetting + repairing A.V. 5-8-9 VILLERS AVENUE ANLEY AVENUE wire entanglement. Day & night work.	
	27th		All sections same as 26th	
	28th		" do	
	29th		" do	
	30th		" do	
	31st		" do	

J. P. Neal Major
for O/C 1/1ST DURHAM FIELD CO. R.E.

4th Division

War Diaries

1/1st Durham Field Coy. R.E.

January to June
1916

4th DIVISION

1/1ST DURHAM FIELD COMPANY.

ROYAL ENGINEERS.

JANUARY 1916.

WAR DIARY
or
INTELLIGENCE SUMMARY

Army Form C. 2118

1/1st DURHAM FIELD CO. R.E.

Place	Date	Hour	Summary of Events and Information	Remarks and references to Appendices
MAILLY	1916 Jany 1st		Nos 1 & 4 Sections on front line trenches at REDAN, CHATHAM & CARDIFF. Dugouts at TENDERLOIN. Day & night work. No 3 Section 2nd line trenches & wiring at AUCHONVILLERS. No 2 Section party of 14 men supervising improvement of huts at ACHEUX & FORCEVILLE. Remainder of Section attached to Nos 1, 3 & 4 Sections for work.	
	2nd		All sections detailed as Jany 1st 1916	
	3rd		— do —	
	4th		— do —	
	5th		Nos 1, 2 & 4 — Same as 1st Jany 1916. No 3 Section commencement of "Bomb Store" at AUCHONVILLERS. 2nd line trenches wiring at AUCHON. Machine Gun emplacement in A.V.S.	

Am Terry Major
O/C 1/1st DURHAM FIELD CO. R.E.

Army Form C. 2118

1/1ST DURHAM FIELD CO. R.E.

WAR DIARY
or
INTELLIGENCE SUMMARY
(Erase heading not required.)

Place	Date	Hour	Summary of Events and Information	Remarks and references to Appendices
MAILLY	Jany 6th		All sections detailed for work as Jany 5th -16.	
	7th		— do — — do — — do —	
	8th		Rest day. General inspection of equipment arms. Training & inspection of the new smoke helmet.	
	9th		Nos 1 & 4 Sections on Front Line trenches at CHATHAM, ROMAN ROAD & BOURDON trenches. Dugouts for N.W.B. battalion Headquarters at TENDERLOIN, Elephant Shelters at BORROW. EGG STREET & POMPADOUR. No 3 Section 2 one line trenches AUCHON - Bomb Store at AUCHON. Elephant Shelter shelter to COR I SEUM & machine gun emplacement. A.V.S. wiring. No 2 Section party of 14 men on improvement of hut town at ACH ELL X, remainder of section detailed for work with nos 1. 3 & 4. Section	

AmDerry Major
O/C

1/1ST DURHAM FIELD CO. R.E.

Army Form C. 2118

WAR DIARY
or
INTELLIGENCE SUMMARY
(Erase heading not required.)

1/1st DURHAM FIELD CO. R.E.

Place	Date	Hour	Summary of Events and Information	Remarks and references to Appendices
MAILLY	Jany 10th 1916		All sections detailed for duty as Jany 9th.	
	11th		do	
	12th		do	
	13th		do	
	14th		do	
	15th		do	
	16th		General inspections of arms & equipment. Foot & Smoke helmet training.	
	17th		No 1 & 4 Sections trenches at CHATHAM, elephant shelters at POMPADOUR and four Lw posts.	
			No 3 Section machine gun emplacements, tombstone, strong AUCHON. Shelters in WITHINGTON. Day night work.	
	18th		No 2 Section. Party 14 men on improvement of Section and roads at ACHEUX, remainder of Section detailed for duty with Nos 1-3-4 Sections.	

AM Derry Major
O/C 1/1st DURHAM FIELD CO. R.E.

WAR DIARY
or
INTELLIGENCE SUMMARY
(Erase heading not required.)

Army Form C. 2118

1/1st DURHAM FIELD CO. R.E.

Place	Date	Hour	Summary of Events and Information	Remarks and references to Appendices
MAILLY	Aug 19th		No 1st Section employed on front line trenches at CHATHAM, front line posts, POM PADOUR Shelter. No 3 Section machine gun emplacement AV 5. preparing ground for ELEPHANT SHELTERS in AV 4. repairing gun emplacement FORTRESS ROAD. Revetting ANLEY TRENCH. Wire entanglements + Bomb Store AUCHON. No 2 Section part of 12 men on improvement of billets and roads at ACHEUX, remainder employed with 1.3 7th (Section)	
	20th		same as above	
	21st		same as above	
	22nd		same as above	
	23rd		same as above	
	24th		Rest day. Inspection of arms equipment &c	

AM Berry Major
O/c 1st Durham Field Co. R.E.

Army Form C. 2118

WAR DIARY
or
INTELLIGENCE SUMMARY
(Erase heading not required.)

1/1ST DURHAM FIELD CO. R.E.

Place	Date	Hour	Summary of Events and Information	Remarks and references to Appendices
MAILLY	January	7.00	1st Section from line trenches CHATHAM	
	25.		Clearing BORDEN trench, Revetting NEW trench, Elephant shelters POMPADOUR & EGG Street, from dug-outs in BROADWAY trench. 1st Av. Day & night work.	
			2nd Section infantry parties.	
			3rd Sect. 13 men improvement of billets & roads at ACHEUX	
			remainder if section with 1, 3 & 4 sections	
			4th Section as stated for 19 – Jany 16.	
	26th		— do — — do — — do —	
	27th		— do — — do — — do —	
	28th		— do — — do — — do —	
	29th		— do — — do — — do —	
	30th	7.00	1st Section as above, and NEW TRENCH in	
	30=		A NEW EGG Street 2nd & 3rd Section & infantry parties	

Am Derry Major
O/C 1st Durham Field Coy RE

Army Form C. 2118

WAR DIARY
or
INTELLIGENCE SUMMARY

(Erase heading not required.)

1/1ST DURHAM FIELD CO. R.E.

Place	Date	Hour	Summary of Events and Information	Remarks and references to Appendices
MAILLY	January 30th		Section 1 & 2 men on improvement of trench & tracks at ACHEUX. remainder of section took 1 & 3 tr sections.	
	31st		No 3 Section. Elephant shell in AV H. Bomb stores at AUCHON. wire entanglements. all sections at stables for 30th June 16—	

Arm. Terry Major
O/C 1st Durham Field Co R.E.

4th DIVISION.

1/1st DURHAM FIELD COMPANY.

ROYAL ENGINEERS.

FEBRUARY 1916.

WAR DIARY
or
INTELLIGENCE SUMMARY
(Erase heading not required.)

Army Form C. 2118.

1/1ST DURHAM FIELD CO. R.E.

Hour, Date, Place	Summary of Events and Information	Remarks and references to Appendices
MAILLY-MAILLET. Feby 1st 1916	Rest day for all sections. Inspection of arms, equipment, smoke helmets etc.	
2nd	Sections employed in collecting stores in trenches, front of the 3 section on Elephant shelter, 2 on gun trenches, for observation post, heavy mortar.	
3rd	Sections collecting stores in trenches to be taken over by 150th Field Coy R.E.	
4th	Company proceeded to MONDICOURT to take over improvement of billets, latrines etc.	
5th	Sections employed in the clearing up of billets. No 1 Section detailed for work at DOULLENS Army Headqrs for improvement of billets etc.	A.W. Derry Major O/C 1st Durham Field Coy R.E.

Army Form C. 2118.

1/1ST DURHAM FIELD CO. R.E.

WAR DIARY
or
INTELLIGENCE SUMMARY

(Erase heading not required.)

Instructions regarding War Diaries and Intelligence Summaries are contained in F. S. Regs., Part II. and the Staff Manual respectively. Title pages will be prepared in manuscript.

Hour, Date, Place	Summary of Events and Information	Remarks and references to Appendices
MONDICOURT.		
July 6th	Church parade.	
7th	Section employed as stated for July 5th	
8th	— do —	
9th	No 1, 3 & 4 Sections proceeded to DOULLENS for the improvement of billets & building of Latrines etc.	
	No 2 Section detained for duty at MONDICOURT.	
10th	Sections detained for duty on improvement of billet accommodation at DOULLENS and MONDICOURT.	
11th	— do — do — do —	

AM Durry Major
O/C 1st Durham Field Co R.E.

Army Form C. 2118.

WAR DIARY
or
INTELLIGENCE SUMMARY
(Erase heading not required.)

1/1ST DURHAM FIELD CO. R.E.

Hour, Date, Place	Summary of Events and Information	Remarks and references to Appendices
DOULLENS. 3 Aug/12.	Nos 1.3 & 4 Sections on work improvement of billet accomodation, Latrines, etc at DOULLENS. No 2 Section fitting bunks for billet accomodation. Latrines stacks at GRENAS.	
	↑ MONDICOURT.	
	1 Lieut J.S. Brown joins Coy today, transferred from 5th Durham Light Infantry.	
13 "	Church parade	
14 "	Sections detailed for work as Aug 12th	
15 "	— do — do	
16 "	— do — do	
17 "	— do — do	
18 "	— do — do	
19 "	— do — do	

Am Derry
Major
OC 1st Durham Field Co.
R.E.

Army Form C. 2118.

1/1st DURHAM FIELD CO. R.E.

WAR DIARY
or
INTELLIGENCE SUMMARY
(Erase heading not required.)

Hour, Date, Place	Summary of Events and Information	Remarks and references to Appendices
DOULLENS. 20/2/16.	Church parade	
21/2/16	Nos 1 & 3 tt. Sections on improvement of billet accomodation. Latrines at DOULLENS.	
22/2/16	No 2 Section billet accomodation. Latrines & Baths at MONDICOURT & GRANAS.	
	2nd Lieut. F.P. CHEVERTON joins Company today from 2nd Tyne. Northumberland F.E.	
23/2/16	Sections detailed for work as 21/2/16	
24/2/16	do	
25/2/16	do	
26/2/16	do	
27/2/16	Church parade & inspection of arms & equipment etc.	Capt Denny Major Officer Commanding 1/1st Northumbrian Field Coy R.E.

Army Form C. 2118.

WAR DIARY
or
INTELLIGENCE SUMMARY
(Erase heading not required.)

1/1ST DURHAM FIELD CO. R.E.

Hour, Date, Place	Summary of Events and Information	Remarks and references to Appendices
DOULLENS 28/5/16	Nos 1 & 3 Sections on improvement of billet accommodation & latrines at DOULLENS. No 2 Section billet accommodation Latrines at MONDICOURT and GRANAS. No 4 section proceeded to LUCHEUX to take over work from West Lancs Field Co.	
29/5/16	Sections detailed for work on billet improvement Latrines at DOULLENS, MONDICOURT, GRANAS, and LUCHEUX.	

Ann Derry Major
O/C 1st Durham Field Co

4th DIVISION.

1/1 DURHAM FIELD COMPANY.

ROYAL ENGINEERS.

MARCH 1916.

Army Form C. 2118.

WAR DIARY
or
INTELLIGENCE SUMMARY

(Erase heading not required.)

1/1ST DURHAM FIELD CO. R.E.

Instructions regarding War Diaries and Intelligence Summaries are contained in F. S. Regs., Part II. and the Staff Manual respectively. Title Pages will be prepared in manuscript.

Place	Date 1916	Hour	Summary of Events and Information	Remarks and references to Appendices
DOULLENS	MARCH 1st		Nos 1. 3 + 4 Sections employed on Billet accommodation Burying of frames, Etc. water mains.	
	2nd		No 2 Section employed at MONDICOURT on billet accommodation, Latrines Etc.	
	3rd		— do — — do — — do —	
	4th		— do — — do — — do —	
	5th		Church parade 10.15 am.	
	6th		Sections on work as detailed for MARCH 1st &c.	
	7th		— do — — do — — do —	
	8th		— do — — do — — do —	
	9th		— do — — do — — do —	
	10th		— do — — do — — do —	

A.W. Jeffery Major
o/c 1/1st DURHAM FIELD CO. R.E.

Army Form C. 2118.

WAR DIARY
or
INTELLIGENCE SUMMARY

(Erase heading not required.)

1/1ST DURHAM FIELD CO. R.E.

Place	Date 1916	Hour	Summary of Events and Information	Remarks and references to Appendices
DOULLENS	March 11th	11—	Nos 1 - 3 & 4th Sections employed on Billet accommodation, erection of Latrines, Baths, water mains.	
	12th		No 2 Section on billet accomodation, erection of Latrines at MONDICOURT	
	13th		Church parade at 10-15 a.m.	
	14th		Sections employed as stated for March 11th & 16	
			— do —	
	15th		— do —	
	16th		— do —	
	17th		— do —	

AWJerry Major
O/C 1/1ST DURHAM FIELD CO. R.E.

Army Form C. 2118.

WAR DIARY
or
INTELLIGENCE SUMMARY
(Erase heading not required.)

1/1st DURHAM FIELD CO. R.E.

Place	Date 1916	Hour	Summary of Events and Information	Remarks and references to Appendices
DOULLENS	MARCH 18th		No 1 Section Headquarters marched from DOULLENS to BAVINCOURT to take over from 153rd Field Cy R.E. No 2 Section marched from MONDICOURT to BIENVILLERS. Nos 3 & 4 Sections marched from DOULLENS to BIENVILLERS.	
	19th		No 4 Section marched from DOULLENS & FONQUEVILLERS to take over work from 153rd Field Cy R.E. No 1 Section Headquarters Church parade. Nos 2, 3 & 4 Sections General fatigues, section officer's visited front line trenches at FONQUEVILLERS.	
	20th		No 1 Section took over workshops at BAVINCOURT for work. Building huts at LA HERLIERE, A.S.C. dump at GRINCOURT. Nos 2, 3 & 4 Sections front line trenches improving & revetting.	

Wm Denny
Major
O/C
1/1st DURHAM FIELD CO. R.E.

Army Form C. 2118.

WAR DIARY
or
INTELLIGENCE SUMMARY

(Erase heading not required.)

1/1st DURHAM FIELD CO. R.E.

Place	Date	Hour	Summary of Events and Information	Remarks and references to Appendices
BAVINCOURT	MARCH 1916 21st		No 1 Section on work at Stops, Huts at LA HERLIERE, A.S.C. Dumps at GRINCOURT. No 2 & 3 Sections front line trenches improving and revetting & Dugouts.	
	22nd		No 1 Section improving revetting front line trenches No 2 Section as stated for march 21st 1916. No 2 Section repairing dugouts in front line No 3 Section building dugouts observation post. No 4 Repairing Dugouts & repairing trenches	
	23rd		All sections same as march 22nd/16	
	24th		All sections same as march 22nd	

AM Denny Major
O.C.
1/1st DURHAM FIELD CO. R.E.

2449 Wt. W14957/M90 750,000 1/16 J.B.C. & A. Forms/C.2118/12.

WAR DIARY
or
INTELLIGENCE SUMMARY

Army Form C. 2118.

1/1ST DURHAM FIELD CO. R.E.

Place	Date	Hour	Summary of Events and Information	Remarks and references to Appendices
BANCOURT	MARCH 25th 1916	6	No 1 Section on shop work, R.S.C. dump at GRINCOURT. Hut at LA HERLIERE. No 2 Section dugouts, revetting front line trenches, deepening of communication trench. No 3 Section Repairs to Divisional Line observation post. No 4 Section repairing dugouts & trenches.	
	26th		No 1 Section as duties for March 25th. No 2 Section ——— do ——— do ———. No 3 Section Dugouts, Observation post, revetting and improving 2nd Line trenches. No 4 Section Same as March 25th.	

A.W. Terry Major
O/C 1/1ST DURHAM FIELD CO. R.E.

Army Form C. 2118.

WAR DIARY
or
INTELLIGENCE SUMMARY

(Erase heading not required.)

1/1ST DURHAM FIELD CO. R.E.

Place	Date	Hour	Summary of Events and Information	Remarks and references to Appendices
BIENVILLERS	MARCH 1916 27th	7-	Headquarters moved from BAVINCOURT to BIENVILLERS.	
			No 1 Section Chute work & A.S.C. Dump at LE HERLERE	
			No 2 Section Dugouts, Dugout repairs, revetting support line	
			No 3 & 4 Sections as stated for 27th March	
	28th		No 1 Section as stated for 27th March	
			No 2 Section Dugouts & Dugout repairs	
			No 3. Section Dugouts, observation post, revetting 2nd line trenches	
			No 4 Section New trench cut to North Fortress, and wired.	
			Night work with infantry parties.	
	29th		No 1 Section as stated for March 27th.	
			No 2 Section Dugouts & Dugout repairs. Pump repairs.	
			No 3 Section Revetting & improving Dwarmed Second line	
			No 4 Section Completion of new trench North Fortress.	
			Lt E.A. Inge joined & Lw Agnes on overmonth	
			protection with a view of transfer.	

A.H. Derry Major
1/1ST DURHAM FIELD CO. R.E.
OC

WAR DIARY or INTELLIGENCE SUMMARY

Army Form C. 2118.

1/1ST DURHAM FIELD CO. R.E.

Place	Date 1916	Hour	Summary of Events and Information	Remarks and references to Appendices
BIENVILLERS	MARCH 30th		No 1 Section available for 27th = 1916. No 2 Section Rest day. General Inspection of Arms, Equipment Etc. No 3 Section Reveting & improving dugouts 2nd line. No 4 Section Rest day General Inspection of arms & Equipment Etc.	
	31st		No 1 Section available for 27th = 1916. No 2 Section Dugouts in front line. No 3 Section Rest day General inspection of arms & equipment. No 4 Section Deepening & widening new trench with fittings	

A.W. Derry Major
O/C 1/1st Durham Field Co. R.E.

4th DIVISION.

1/1ST DURHAM FIELD COMPANY.

ROYAL ENGINEERS.

APRIL 1916.

Army Form C. 2118.

WAR DIARY
or
INTELLIGENCE SUMMARY
(Erase heading not required.)

1/1ST DURHAM FIELD CO. R.E.

Place	Date 1916	Hour	Summary of Events and Information	Remarks and references to Appendices
BIENVILLERS	April 1st		No 1 Section employed on Workshops at BAVINCOURT. Also dump at AYRINCOURT. Erecting pumps &troughs at LEHEILLIERE. No 2 Section dugout nets in BERLIN St, WARWICK AV. CHISWICK AV. LULU LANE. No 3 Section. Personnel Armt [?] for repairing Netting Trenches, Machine Gun emplacements T.65. Approving dugouts for R.H.A. No 4 Section at FONQUEVILLERS, improving revetment revetting wire entanglements	
	2nd		Same as stated for April 1st	
	3rd		do	do
	4th		do	do
	5th		do	do

J.R. Muir
Major

WAR DIARY
or
INTELLIGENCE SUMMARY

(Erase heading not required.)

Army Form C. 2118.

1/1ˢᵀ DURHAM FIELD CO. R.E.

Place	Date	Hour	Summary of Events and Information	Remarks and references to Appendices
In the field	April 6		No 1 Section as detailed for April 1ˢᵗ	
			Nos 2 & 3 ⋅⋅ Section rest day inspection of equipment Arms & Co.	
	7		Same as detailed for April 1ˢᵗ	
	8		— do — — do —	
	9		— do — — do —	
	10		No 1 Section shop work at BAVIN COURT. H.Q. Divisional Laundry at WARLIN COURT. Repairing huts at GAUDIEN PRÉ	
			No 2 Section dugouts BERLIN St. WARWICK AV. CHISWICK AV. LULU LANE. or HANNES CAMP §1. Reopening MONCHY ROAD.	
			No 3 Section. Divisional 2ⁿᵈ Line revetting repairing trenches. M.G. emplacement T.6.8. Supervising erection of dugouts for R.F.A.	
			No 4 Section revetting & cutting firesteps NEWLAND FOIV QUEVILLERS and hkurttin R.B. ROSE AV. trench.	R.B. Kerr Major

Army Form C. 2118.

WAR DIARY
or
INTELLIGENCE SUMMARY

1/1ST DURHAM FIELD CO. R.E.

(Erase heading not required.)

Instructions regarding War Diaries and Intelligence Summaries are contained in F. S. Regs., Part II. and the Staff Manual respectively. Title Pages will be prepared in manuscript.

Place	Date	Hour	Summary of Events and Information	Remarks and references to Appendices
In the field	April			
	11th		All Sections on Establ. for April 10 =	
	12th		Res day. Inspection of Equipment Arms etc.	
	13th		All Sections on duties for April 10 =	
	14th		— do —	
	15th		— do —	
	16th		— do —	
	17th		— do —	
	18th		— do —	
	19th		— do —	
	20th		— do —	
	21st		Res day. Inspection of Equipment, Arms &c.	J.R. Kerr Major

WAR DIARY or INTELLIGENCE SUMMARY

Army Form C. 2118.

1/1ST DURHAM FIELD CO. R.E.

Place	Date	Hour	Summary of Events and Information	Remarks and references to Appendices
In the field	April 22		No 1 Section workshops at BAVINCOURT. 4th Nov Laundry WAR LIN court Huts at LA HERLIERE, Running R.F.A. dump to HUMBERCAMP.	
			No 2 Section. Dugouts at HANNESCAMPS. Regimental Aid post. Elephant Station for R.A.M.C.	
			No 3 Section revetting emplacement of duramens second line trenches. M.G. emplacement T.65. Observed post in second line, and dugouts for R.F.A.	
			No 4 Section at FONQUEVILLERS, revetting R.E.R.E. air building Traverse. Snipers opposite. Cleaning new trench.	
	23		— do — — do —	
	24		— do — — do —	
	25		— do — — do —	
	26		— do — — do —	
	27		— do — — do —	

J. R. Neil
Major

Army Form C. 2118.

WAR DIARY
or
INTELLIGENCE SUMMARY

(Erase heading not required.)

1/1ST DURHAM FIELD CO. R.E.

Instructions regarding War Diaries and Intelligence Summaries are contained in F. S. Regs., Part II. and the Staff Manual respectively. Title Pages will be prepared in manuscript.

Place	Date	Hour	Summary of Events and Information	Remarks and references to Appendices
Intke fires	Apl 28th		All Sections employed as stated for 22nd	
	29th		— do —	
	30th		— do —	

J.R. Weir, Major

4th DIVISION.

I/Ist DURHAM FIELD COMPANY.

ROYAL ENGINEERS.

MAY 1916.

Army Form C. 2118

WAR DIARY
or
INTELLIGENCE SUMMARY
(Erase heading not required.)

1/1ST DURHAM FIELD CO. R.E.

Place	Date 1916	Hour	Summary of Events and Information	Remarks and references to Appendices
In the Field	May 1st		Nos 1 Section at BAVINCOURT. on shopwork Etc, Laundry at WARLINCOURT.	
			Nos 2 & 3 Sections at BIENVILLERS. rest day, inspection of arms, equipment Etc.	
			No 4 at FONQUEVILLERS. rest day inspection of equipment Etc.	
	May 2nd		All Sections preparing for move on following day.	
	May 3rd		No 1 Section marched from BAVINCOURT to CAUMESNIL) for breaking and Nos 2 & 3 marched from BIENVILLERS) Headquarters. No 4 marched from FONQUEVILLERS	
	May 4th		Company parade for company training services.	
	5th		— do — — do — — do —	

Amiens
Major
OC. 1st Durham Field Coy R.E.

Army Form C. 2118.

1/1st DURHAM FIELD CO. R.E.

WAR DIARY
or
INTELLIGENCE SUMMARY
(Erase heading not required.)

Hour, Date, Place	Summary of Events and Information	Remarks and references to Appendices
In the field. May 6th 1916	Nos 1 & 4 sections marched to BEAUMETZ to be attached to 1/1st Renfrewshire Field Coy R.E. for work and discipline. Nos 2 & 3 sections company training there. Preparing for move following day.	
May 7th	Nos 2 & 3 sections Headquarters marched from CAUMESNIL to BERTRANCOURT. Nos 1 & 2 sections of 1/1st Renfrewshire Field Coy R.E. attached at BERTRANCOURT to be attached for work & discipline.	
May 8th	Officers, NCOs marking trenches at COLINCAMPS & MAILLY for commencement of work. Sections cleaning billets etc.	

AW Dean Major
O/C 1st Durham Field Coy R.E.

Army Form C. 2118.

1/1st DURHAM FIELD CO. R.E.

WAR DIARY
or
INTELLIGENCE SUMMARY
(Erase heading not required.)

Instructions regarding War Diaries and Intelligence Summaries are contained in F.S. Regs., Part II. and the Staff Manual respectively. Title pages will be prepared in manuscript.

Hour, Date, Place	Summary of Events and Information	Remarks and references to Appendices
In the field May 9th 1916	Nos 2 & 3 Sections & attached Sections on work in 3rd H. & S. AVENUES on new communication trench cut, old communication trench deepened & berm cleared & parapets improved, 12 new Traverses commenced. CRESCENT trench deepened and improved for cover, ROMAN ROAD berm cleared and drainage cut. DELANNEY & CHEERO deepened & improved for cover. Infantry parties provided night working.	
10th	do do	
11th	No 1 Section attacked VAUCHELLES for Hut building. do	
12th	do do	
13th	do do	
14th	do do	

A. N. Dixon
Major
O/C 1st Durham Field Coy R.E.

1247 W 3299 200,000 (E) 8/14 J.B.C. & A.   Forms/C. 2118/11.

Army Form C. 2118.

1/1st DURHAM FIELD CO. R.E.

WAR DIARY
or
INTELLIGENCE SUMMARY
(Erase heading not required.)

Instructions regarding War Diaries and Intelligence Summaries are contained in F. S. Regs, Part II. and the Staff Manual respectively. Title pages will be prepared in manuscript.

Hour, Date, Place	Summary of Events and Information	Remarks and references to Appendices
In the field May 15th 1916	No 1 Section, hut at VAUCHELLES. No 2, 3 & 4 attached Sections supervising infantry parties on 3rd, 4th Avenues, deepening & preparing for trench boards. 3rd Avenue tramway improves. TAUPIN & VALADE deepened & cleaned. HIGH HOLBORN, DELAWNEY, CHEERO, trench deepening, improving for cover. Supervising BOMB STORE in quarry SUCRERIE, SUNKEN ROAD. Driving gallery for NEW Brigade HEADQTRS in ROMAN ROAD. Trueing R.A.M.C. Shed in 5th AV. by mining. Building RATION DUMP in Orchard, SUCRERIE ROAD. Cutting O.P. for 11th Infantry Bde in VALADE. Preparing buildings for proposed H.Q. offices.	A M Dean major Offr 1/1st Durham Field Coy R.E.

Forms/C. 2118/11.

Army Form C. 2118.

1/1ST DURHAM FIELD CO. R.E.

WAR DIARY
or
INTELLIGENCE SUMMARY
(Erase heading not required.)

Hour, Date, Place	Summary of Events and Information	Remarks and references to Appendices
In the field May 16th 1916	Sections on work same as 15th May.	
17th	Sections on work, same as 15th May. No 4 Section arrived at BERTRANCOURT, detached from 1/1st Renfrewshire Field Coy. R.E.	
18th	No 2, 3 & 4 Sections marched MAILLY-IN-MILLET to billet. No 1 Section on further building at VAUCHELLES.	
19th	All Sections employed as stated for work on 18th May.	
20th	All Sections employed as stated for work on 18th May.	

AWDean
Major
O/C 1st Durham Field Coy R.E.

Army Form C. 2118.

2/1st DURHAM FIELD CO. R.E.

WAR DIARY
or
INTELLIGENCE SUMMARY
(Erase heading not required.)

Hour, Date, Place	Summary of Events and Information	Remarks and references to Appendices
In the field May 21st 1916	No 1 Section erecting Huts at VAUCHELLES Nos 2, 3, 4 Sections, and attached Section deepening & cleaning trenches in 4th & 5th AV. R.A.M.C. Dugouts 5th AV. & SUNKEN ROAD. BOMB Store at SACRERIE, Ration Dump in Orchard at SACRERIE, O.P. in VALADE trench & advanced Headquarters at BERTRANCOURT. Battalion Headquarters in ROMAN-ROAD.	
22nd	— do — — do — — do —	
23.	— do — — do — — do —	

Ami Jerry Major
Офр. 2nd Durham Field Cy R.E.

Army Form C. 2118.

1/1st DURHAM FIELD CO. R.E.

WAR DIARY
or
INTELLIGENCE SUMMARY
(Erase heading not required.)

Place	Hour, Date	Summary of Events and Information	Remarks and references to Appendices
In the field	May 24th 1916	No. 1 Section erecting Huts at VAUCHELLES.	
		Nos 2, 3 rd Sections Cutting R.A.M.C. shells S-AV. Bomb Store, SUCRERIE, Rake dump, SUCRERIE, preparing observation post in VALADE trench Brigade Headquarters dugout in RONTAN ROAD. Burning diamond Headquarters sanitary for R.A.M.C. shells BERTRANCOURT.	
		Attached Section Cutting gazing under SUNKEN ROAD cutting for Corps O.P. in S. AV.	
	May 25th	— do — — do — — do —	
	26	No 2 Section Rear Day. Inspection of Arms etc. Nos 1 - 3 rd + attached Section as detailed for 24th May.	
	27th	All Sections on works as stated for May 24th	

Ann Denny
Major
1/1st Durham Field Co R.E.

Army Form C. 2118.

1/1st DURHAM FIELD CO. R.E.

WAR DIARY
or
INTELLIGENCE SUMMARY
(Erase heading not required.)

Hour, Date, Place	Summary of Events and Information	Remarks and references to Appendices
In the field May 1916.	No 1 Section Erecting huts at VAUCHELLES. No 2, 3 rt Sections R.A.M.C Shelter in St AN. Bombstore at SCORRIE, O.P. in VALADE Trench. Cellar dump in ORCHARD. Brigade Headquarters in RONDAN ROAD, R.A.M.C dugout shelters. Divisional Head quarters at BERTRAN COURT. Attached Section forming gallery under SUNKEN RD. Corps O.P. in St AV.	
29th	do — do — do — do — do —	
30th	do — do — do — do — do —	
31.	do — do — do — do — do —	

AW Irwin Major
O/C 1st Durham Field Co R.E.

4th DIVISION.

1/1ST DURHAM FIELD COMPANY.

ROYAL ENGINEERS.

JUNE 1916.

Army Form C. 2118

WAR DIARY
or
INTELLIGENCE SUMMARY

1/1st Durham Field Coy, R.E. (T).

(*Erase heading not required.*)

Place	Date	Hour	Summary of Events and Information	Remarks and references to Appendices
In the Field.	1916. June 1st.		No 1 Section - moved from VAUCHELLES to BERTRANCOURT.	
			No 2 Section - cutting chamber and galleries for R.A.M.C. shelter at MAILLY and SUNKEN ROAD.	
			Nos 3 & 4 Sections - Rest day - inspections of arms, equipment etc, R.A.M.C. shelter and building of huts for Divisional Headquarters at BERTRANCOURT.	
			Attached section from RENFREWSHIRE Field Coy, R.E. rest day.	
	June 2nd.		No 1 Section - moved from BERTRANCOURT to MAILLY-MAILLET.	
			No 2 section - rest day - inspection of arms and equipment etc, less men on R.A.M.C. shelters at MAILLY and SUNKEN ROAD.	
			No 3 Section - bomb store at SUCRERIE, O.P. for 11th Brigade in VALLADE trench, O.P. for Army Range sounding, Ration dump in ORCHARD.	
			No 4 Section - 12th Brigade Headquarters in ROMAN ROAD, R.A.M.C. shelter and huts for Divisional Headquarters at BERTRANCOURT.	
			Attached section on Corps O.P. in 5th AVENUE.	

(illegible signature) Major,
O/C 1st Durham Field Coy, R.E.

Army Form C. 2118.

WAR DIARY
or
INTELLIGENCE SUMMARY

(Erase heading not required.)

1/1st Durham Field Coy, R.E.

Instructions regarding War Diaries and Intelligence Summaries are contained in F. S. Regs., Part II. and the Staff Manual respectively. Title Pages will be prepared in manuscript.

Place	Date	Hour	Summary of Events and Information	Remarks and references to Appendices
In the Field.	1916. June 3rd.		Sections on work as follows :- Divisional O.P., Signal O.P., 11th Brigade O.P., Army O.P., R.A.M.C. shelter in 5th AV. SUNKEN ROAD, and MAILLY, Bomb store at SUCRERIE, Ration dump in ORCHARD, 12th Brigade Headquarters in ROMAN ROAD, building trench bridges at MAILLY, RAMC shelter and Divisional headquarters huts at BERTRANCOURT. Attached section Corps O.P. in 5th AV. SUNKEN ROAD.	
	June 4th		------do-------- -------do--------	
	" 5th		------do-------- -------do-------- Attached section rejoins own Unit.	
	" 6th		------do-------- -------do--------	
	" 7th		------do-------- -------do--------	
	" 8th		No 3 Section rest day, remainder of sections on work as above for June 3rd.	
	" 9th		All sections on work as stated for June 3rd.	
	" 10th		All sections on work as stated for June 3rd.	
	" 11th		All sections on work as stated for June 3rd.	

[signature] Major,
O/C 1st Durham Field Coy, R.E.

Army Form C. 2118.

WAR DIARY
or
INTELLIGENCE SUMMARY

(Erase heading not required.)

1/1st Durham Field Coy, R.E. (T)

Instructions regarding War Diaries and Intelligence Summaries are contained in F. S. Regs, Part II and the Staff Manual respectively. Title Pages will be prepared in manuscript.

Place	Date	Hour	Summary of Events and Information	Remarks and references to Appendices
In the Field.	1916 June 12th.		Sections on work as follows :- Divisional O.P., Signals O.P., 11th Brigade O.P., Army O.P., making trench bridges, R.A.M.C. shelters at 5th A.V. SUNKEN ROAD, MAILLY and BERTRANCOURT, Rations dump in ORCHARD, 11th Brigade Headquarters in BOW STREET, 12th Brigade Headquarters in ROMAN ROAD, building Divisional Headquarters huts at BERTRANCOURT.	
	" 13th		------------------do------------------	
	" 14th		------------------do------------------	
	" 15th		------------------do------------------	
			iiLieut E.H. TRIGGS, seconded to 4th Divisional Signals R.E.	
	" 16th		Sections on work as follows :- Divisional O.P., Signals O.P., 11th Brigade O.P., Army O.P., making trench bridges at MAILLY, R.A.M.C. shelters at 5th AV. SUNKEN ROAD, MAILLY, SUCRERIE, 5th A.V. WEST END, and WATLING STREET, 11th Brigade Headquarters at BOW STREET, 12th Brigade headquarters in ROMAN ROAD, ration dump in ORCHARD, building Divisional Headquarters huts and dugout at BERTRANCOURT.	
	" 17th		Same as stated for June 16th.	
	" 18th		Same as stated for June 16th.	
	" 19th		Same as stated for June 16th.	
	" 20th		Same as stated for June 16th.	
	" 21st		Same as stated for June 16th.	

AW Deer
Major,
O/C 1st Durham Field Coy, R.E.

Army Form C. 2118.

1/1st Durham Field Coy, R.E.

WAR DIARY
or
INTELLIGENCE SUMMARY

(Erase heading not required.)

Instructions regarding War Diaries and Intelligence Summaries are contained in F.S. Regs., Part II. and the Staff Manual respectively. Title Pages will be prepared in manuscript.

Place	Date	Hour	Summary of Events and Information	Remarks and references to Appendices
In the Field.	1916. June 22nd		Sections on work as follows :- Divisional O.P., Signals O.P., R.A.M.C. Shelters in 5th Avenue SUNKEN ROAD, MAILLY, SUCRORIE, 5th AVENUE WEST END, Army O.P. 11th Brigade O.P. 12th Brigade Headquarters ROMAN ROAD, Trench bridges MAILLY, Divisional Headquarters Dugout at BERTRANCOURT.	
	23rd.		Divisional O.P., Signals O.P., 11th Brigade O.P., Army O.P.,) all R.A.M.C. Shelters in 5th AVENUE SUNKEN ROAD, MAILLY, SUCRERIE, 5th AVENUE WEST END) completed. Ration dump in ORCHARD, 12th Brigade Headquarters, ROMAN ROAD. Trench bridges. Divisional Headquarters, BERTRANCOURT, placing last element and fitting headcover.	
	24th.		Nos 1, 2, 3, & 4 Sections moved from MAILLY-MAILLET to BERTRANCOURT.	
	25th.		Company Rest day, general inspection of equipment, arms, iron rations, and smoke helmets. Deficiencies adjusted.	
	26th.		Sections on work as follows :- Headquarters dugout at BERTRANCOURT, and building trench bridges, fitting WARNER PUMP for water supply in BERTRANCOURT, 2 sappers attending to upkeep of pipes in trenches and watersupply, 2 sappers attending to bridges in trenches. No 2 Section resting.	
	27th		--------------------do------------------	
	28th		Headquarters dugout completed, carrying on work as stated for 26th.	
	29th		Same as stated for 26th.	
	30th		Same as stated for 26th.	

AmDerry Major,
O/C 1st Durham Field Coy, R.E.

4th Division

War Diaries

1/1st Durham Field Coy R.E.

July to December 1916

4th DIVISION.

1/1ST DURHAM FIELD COMPANY.

ROYAL ENGINEERS.

JULY 1916.

Army Form C. 2118.

WAR DIARY
or
INTELLIGENCE SUMMARY
(Erase heading not required.)

1/1st Durham Field Coy, R.E.

Instructions regarding War Diaries and Intelligence Summaries are contained in F. S. Regs., Part II. and the Staff Manual respectively. Title Pages will be prepared in manuscript.

Place	Date	Hour	Summary of Events and Information	Remarks and references to Appendices
BERTRAN- COURT.	July 1st 1916.	4.30 a.m.	Nos 1 & 4 Sections moved from BERTRANCOURT to MAILLY-MAILLET for patrol of roads, pipe lines for trench water supply, laying roads and marking routes for motor lorries, from SERRE ROAD to German Lines, and repairs to trench bridges.	
		8 am	No 2 Section under Lieut. J. AITKEN detailed for duty with 11th Infantry Brigade during operation. Moved from NEWGATE STREET to VALADE TRENCH.	
		9.10	Reported to Officer Commanding 11th Infantry Brigade at the LYCEUM, who gave instructions for the section to be moved forward to the German lines, one half being directed to the North flank and the other half to the Southern flank.	
			The O.C. Section accompanied the Brigadier forward. The Brigadier was killed at the entrance of CAT STREET. The O.C. Section then went back to find the Brigade Major. Owing to the German barrage and Machine Gun fire it was not possible to get any messages through from the advanced troops, and the R.E. Section remained out of touch. Eventually Serjeant PETERSEN and 6 men found their way back and reported that they had gone forward with the 11th Brigade. At about 3.30 pm. they established themselves in a shell hole in the parapet of the 3rd German line and held this with bombs and rifle fire for about 2 hours. They retired again about 6.50 p.m. and reached our front line at 7.30 p.m.	
			Casualties as follows :-	
			1 killed.	
			8 wounded.	
			10 missing.	
			No 3 Section at BERTRANCOURT, upkeep and repair of roads from BERTRANCOURT to railway crossing BEAUSSART, erecting pump for water supply for baths, cooking and drinking purposes.	

AMcDerry Major,
O/C 1st Durham Field Coy, R.E.

Army Form C. 2118.

WAR DIARY
or
INTELLIGENCE SUMMARY

(Erase heading not required.)

1/1st Durham Field Coy, R.E.

Hour, Date, Place	Summary of Events and Information	Remarks and references to Appendices
In the Field. July 1st 1916.	Nos 1 & 4 Sections moved from BERTRANCOURT to MAILLY-MAILLET at 4-30 am, for patrol of roads, and pipe lines for water supply, trenches, laying roads and marking routes for motor lorries from SERRE ROAD to GERMAN LINES, and repairs to trench bridges. No 2 Section arrived at point of assembly, NEWGATE STREET, in K.33.A.at 8-10 am, reporting to Officer Commanding 11th Infantry Brigade at the LYCEUM at 9-10am, for duty as instructions issued. No 3 Section at BERTRANCOURT, upkeep and repair of roads from BERTRANCOURT to railway crossing BEAUSSART, erecting pump for water supply to BATHS and drinking and cooking purposes.	
July 2nd.	Nos 1 & 4 Sections repairing roads from MAILLY-MAILLET to SUCRERIE, repairs to pipe line for trench water supply. No 2 Section returned from trenches to BERTRANCOURT for rest. No 3 Section fixing pump for the Watersupply to Baths etc., and road patrol from BERTRANCOURT to to railway crossing BEAUSSART	
July 3rd.	Nos 1 & 4 Sections on water supply for trenches, repairs to pipe line. No 2 Section resting. No 3 Section erection of pump for waterservice BERTRANCOURT, making crosses for graves at MAILLY-MAILLET, and repair of roads.	
July 4th	Nos 1 & 4 Sections on trench water supply service, improving trenches village defences of MAILLY-MAILLET. No 2 Section resting. Erecting pump and tank for water service BERTRANCOURT, repair sto roads, making wooden crosses for graves at MAILLY MAILLET.	

Am Derry Major,
O/C 1st Durham Field Coy, R.E.

Army Form C. 2118.

WAR DIARY
INTELLIGENCE SUMMARY
(Erase heading not required.)

1/1st Durham Field Coy, R.E.

Instructions regarding War Diaries and Intelligence Summaries are contained in F. S. Regs., Part II. and the Staff Manual respectively. Title Pages will be prepared in manuscript.

Place	Date	Hour	Summary of Events and Information	Remarks and references to Appendices
	July 5th 1916.		Nos 1 & 4 Sections on Trench water supply and repairs to pipe line, improving trenches for village defences at MAILLY-MAILLET. Nos 2 & 3 Sections Erection of pump for watersupply at BERTRANCOURT completed., repairs to roads at BERTRANCOURT, and erection of baths.	
	July 6th 1916.		------do------	
	" 7th 1916.		Nos 1 & 4 Sections cutting NEW TRENCH in 5TH AVENUE, repairs to road from BERTRANCOURT to SUCRERIE, fencing in cemetery at SUCRERIE, patroling pipe lines for trench water supply. Nos 2 & 3 Sections erection of baths at BERTRANCOURT, road repairs , fencing in cemetery at BERTRANCOURT, erecting engine for pump for water service.	
	" 8th.		------do------	
	" 9th.		------do------	
	" 10th.		------do------	
	" 11th		------do------ Lieut. L. Robson admitted to 12th Field Ambulance. Lieut. S. Pearson joins company from 2nd Line.	

AinDery Major,
O/C 1st Durham Field Coy, R.E.

Army Form C. 2118.

WAR DIARY
or
INTELLIGENCE SUMMARY

(Erase heading not required.)

1/1st Durham Field Coy, R.E.

Instructions regarding War Diaries and Intelligence Summaries are contained in F. S. Regs., Part II. and the Staff Manual respectively. Title Pages will be prepared in manuscript.

Place	Date	Hour	Summary of Events and Information	Remarks and references to Appendices
July	12th 1916.		Nos 1 & 4 Sections Revetting newtrench in SUNKEN ROAD, machine gun emplacement in 6th AVENUE, trench water supply, road repairs from BERTRANCOURT to SUCRERIE. Nos 2 & 3 Sections road repairs in BERTRANCOURT, watersupply and attending to engines and pumps at BERTRANCOURT and BUS, erecting baths at BERTRANCOURT, fencing in cemetery at BEAUSSART.	
	13th		-----------do------------do------------do------------	
	14th		No 1 Section rest day, inspection of arms, equipment etc, remainder of sections as detailed for 12th. Lieut. R.W. WILLIAMS and 1iLieut. H.H.GRAY joins Company from 2nd Line.	
	15th		No 4 Section rest day, inspections of arms, equipment etc, remainder of sectons as detailed for 12th.	
	16th.		Same as detailed for 12th.	
	17th		Same as detailed for 12th.	

A.W.Derry
Major,
O/C 1st Durham Field Coy, R.E.

Army Form C. 2118.

WAR DIARY

INTELLIGENCE SUMMARY

(Erase heading not required.)

Instructions regarding War Diaries and Intelligence Summaries are contained in F. S. Regs., Part II. and the Staff Manual respectively. Title Pages will be prepared in manuscript.

1/1st Durham Field Coy, R.E.

Place	Date	Hour	Summary of Events and Information	Remarks and refences to Appendices
	July 18th 1916.		Nos 1 & 4 Sections deepening and widening new trench and dugouts in SUNKEN ROAD, machine gun emplacement in 6th AVENUE, road repairs from BERTRANCOURT to SUCRERIE, water supply in trenches. Nos 2 & 3 Sections erection of Latrines and ablution benches for reinforcement camps near BERTRANCOURT, water supply and attending to pumps and engines at BERTRANCOURT and BUS.	
	19th.		------do------ ------do------ ------do------ repairing roads in BERTRANCOURT.	
	20th.		------do------ ------do------ ------do------	
	21st		Nos 1 & 4 Sections moved from MAILLY-MAILLET to BUS. Headquarters, and Nos 2 & 3 Sections moved from BERTRANCOURT to BUS, relieved by 70th Field Coy, R.E. at 9-0 am.	
	22nd.	8-0am.	Company moved from BUS to AMPLIER, halted for the night.	
	23rd.	8-0 am	Moved from AMPLIER to DOULLENS to entrain for CASSEL at 2-45 pm, arriving at 7-0 pm, marched to CASSEL VILLAGE and rested till 4-30 am. 24/7/16.	
	24th	5-0 am.	Moved from CASSEL VILLAGE to HOUTKERQUE arriving at 8-45 am.	
	25th	2-0 pm	Moved from HOUTKERQUE to POPERINGHE, arriving 4-30 pm, halted at camp for night at L4 a 8.4	
	26th.	11-0 am.	Moved from Camp XX L4 a 8. 4 to PESELHOEK CAMP to relieve 55th Field Coy, R.E. Headquarters and No 4 Section to billet and for work.	
		8-0pm.	Nos 1, 2, & 3 Sections moved from PESELHOEK CAMP to billet and for work on CANAL BANK.	
			1i Lieut. G.V. HURD joins company from 2nd Line.	

Ann Perry
Major,
O/C 1st Durham Field Coy, R.E.

2449 Wt. W14957/M90 750,000 1/16 J.B.C. & A. Forms/C.2118/12.

Army Form C. 2118.

WAR DIARY

INTELLIGENCE SUMMARY

1/1st Durham Field Coy, R.E.

(Erase heading not required.)

Hour, Date, Place	Summary of Events and Information	Remarks and references to Appendices
JULY 27th 1916.	Nos 1, 2, & 3 Sections taking over work from 55th Field Coy, R.E. at CANAL BANK. No 4 Section cleaning billets, and moving into billets taken over from 55th Field Coy, R.E.	
28th 1916.	No 1 Section pumping an clearing site for Medical Aid Post in HUDDERSFIELD ROAD, New Company Headquarters in HEADINGLY LANE. No 2 Section repairing bridges and laying trench boards to approaches. No 3 Section on Trench drainage xxx scheme. No 4 Section General fatigues in Camp, attending to engines for baths at COUTHOVE.	
29th 1916.	No 1 Section repairing light railway HALIFAX ROAD to LANCASHIRE FARM, work completed. Dugout for Trench Mortar Officers on the NILE. Making door and fixing trench boards in communication trench for New Company Headquarters, HEADINGLY LANE. No 2 Section Repairing and improving approaches to bridges. No 3 Section cutting new fire trench to E.28. trench drainage scheme. No 4 Section general duties and Camp fatigues.	
30th 1916.	---------do--------- ---------do---------	
31st 1916	No 1Section completed dugout for Trench Mortar Officers.	

A.W. Derry, Major,
O/C 1st Durham Field Coy, R.E.

4th DIVISION.

1/1ST DURHAM FIELD COMPANY.

ROYAL ENGINEERS.

AUGUST 1916.

WAR DIARY

BY

The Officer Commanding, 1/1st Durham Field Coy, R.E. for the Month of

AUGUST 1916.

Army Form C. 2118.

WAR DIARY
or
INTELLIGENCE SUMMARY.
(Erase heading not required.)

1/1st DURHAM FIELD COY, R.E. (t).

Instructions regarding War Diaries and Intelligence Summaries are contained in F. S. Regs., Part II. and the Staff Manual respectively. Title pages will be prepared in manuscript.

Place	Date	Hour	Summary of Events and Information	Remarks and references to Appendices
	1916. AUGUST.			
PESELHOEK Camp.	1st		Nos 1, 2, & 3 Sections billeted at CANAL BANK., on works as follows :- Dugouts for Company Headquarters, relaying loophole to machine gun emplacement. Dugouts at NEW FARGATE STREET,	
A.20.b.8.3. and Canal Bank.			New trench to E.28 to junction of YORK &WHITE TRENCH, trench cut through and communication established, Dugout on WEST SIDE of CANAL, trench drainage scheme. No 4 Section laying concrete floor in Divisional baths, laying filter bed and building latrines at COUTHOVE laundry, repairs to company transport. 1i Lieut J.S. BROWN attached to Second Army, School of Instruction. Major J.B. HALL attached to C.R.E. 4th Division for duty.	
	2nd		Nos 1, 2, & 3 sections, building sandbag wall on East bank of G.W. bridge, repairing tracks on WINDOOR tramlines and LANCASHIRE FARM line, completing dugouts for Headquarters, preparing Medical Aid Post., Dugouts in FARGATE STREET, new trench to E.28, dugouts on West side of CANAL BANK, and trench drainage scheme. No. 4 Section same as August 1st.	

A.W. Perry, Major,
O/C 1st Durham Field Coy, R. E.

Army Form C. 2118.

WAR DIARY
or
INTELLIGENCE SUMMARY.
(Erase heading not required.)

1/1st DURHAM FIELD COY, R.E. (t).

Instructions regarding War Diaries and Intelligence Summaries are contained in F. S. Regs., Part II. and the Staff Manual respectively. Title pages will be prepared in manuscript.

Place	Date	Hour	Summary of Events and Information	Remarks and references to Appendices
PESBELHOEK Camp.	1916 August			
A.20.b.8.8. and CANAL BANK.	3rd.		C.13.d.5.7. C.13.d.7.5. Forward Sections, Dugouts in FARGATE STREET, Medical Aid Post, making cupboards for bridge demolitions and petrol, repairing tracks on LANCASHIRE LINE, making roadway on West bank and East bank to new bridge, new trench to E.28. trench drainage scheme, completing dugouts West side of CANAL BANK. Back section, laying filter beds and erecting latrines at COUTHOVE laundry, fixing ventilators in Divisional Baths, erecting and fixing pack stores at PROVEN, repairs to company transport.	
	4th		---------do---------- ---------do----------	
	5th		---------do---------- ---------do----------	

Alin Dent Major,
O/C 1st Durham Field Coy, R.E.

Army Form C. 2118.

WAR DIARY
or
INTELLIGENCE SUMMARY. 1/1st DURHAM FIELD COY. R.E.

(Erase heading not required.)

Instructions regarding War Diaries and Intelligence Summaries are contained in F. S. Regs., Part II. and the Staff Manual respectively. Title pages will be prepared in manuscript.

Place	Date	Hour	Summary of Events and Information	Remarks and references to Appendices
PESELHOEK Camp A.20.b.8.8 and CANAL BANK.	1916. August 6th.		Forward Sections, Dugouts in FARGATE STREET C.13.a.3.7. Medical Aid Post at C.13.d.7.5. making and fixing cupboards for bridge demolitions and petrol, building new bridge at 6.W. trench drainage system, excavating and revetting new trench from BARNSLEY ROAD to E.28, completing dugout at CANAL BANK. C.13.c.1.6. Back Section, building incinerator, latrines, and laying filter beds at COUTHOVE laundry, erecting pack stores at PROVEN, and repairs to company transport.	
	7th		------------do------------do------------	
	8th		Casualties 1 N.C.O. and 1 man wounded. Sections on work same as 6th.	

AWDean
Major,
O/C 1st Durham Field Coy, R.E.

T.131. W1. W768-776. 500090. 4/15. Sir J. C. & S.

Army Form C. 2118.

WAR DIARY
or
INTELLIGENCE SUMMARY.   1/1st DURHAM FIELD COY. R.E.
(Erase heading not required.)

Instructions regarding War Diaries and Intelligence Summaries are contained in F. S. Regs., Part II. and the Staff Manual respectively. Title pages will be prepared in manuscript.

Place	Date	Hour	Summary of Events and Information	Remarks and references to Appendices
PESELHOEK Camp. A.20.b.8.8. and CANAL BANK.	1916 August. 9th		Forward Sections, dugouts in FARGATE STREET C.13.a.3.7. Medical Aid Post at C.13.d.7.5. making and fixing cupboards for demolitions and petrol, building new bridge at C.13.c.2.3. trench drainage scheme, dugout for 126th Battery, R.F.A. at C.19.a.8.9. Back section, building incinerator, and latrines, and filter bed at COUTHOVE laundry, erecting drying shed, and pack stores at PROVEN, repairs to company transport. 11 Lieut. G.H.GRAY admitted to 10th Field Ambulance, draft from No 2 Territorial Base, ROUEN of 2 N.C.O's and 9 men.	
	10th		Sections on work as stated for 9th.	
	11th		Sections on work as stated for 9th. No 1section relieved No 1 section at CANAL BANK at 9-20 pm.	
	12th		Forward Sections on work as stated for 9th, and emplacment for Heavy Trench Mortar Battery, at B.12.d.9½.½.	

Oliv Derry Major,
O/C 1st Durham Field Coy, R.E.

Army Form C. 2118.

WAR DIARY
or
INTELLIGENCE SUMMARY.
(Erase heading not required.)

1/1st DURHAM FIELD COY, R.E.

Instructions regarding War Diaries and Intelligence Summaries are contained in F. S. Regs., Part II. and the Staff Manual respectively. Title pages will be prepared in manuscript.

Place	Date	Hour	Summary of Events and Information	Remarks and references to Appendices
	1916. August			
PESELHOEK Camp and A.20.b.8.8. and CANAL BANK.	13th		Forward Sections, Dugouts in FARGATE STREET C.13.a.3.7. Medical Aid Post at C.13.d.7.5. cutting Fusilier communication trench, building new bridge at C.13.c.2.3. repairing and patrolling bridges, Recovering and revetting STIRLING trench, C.14.c.d., trench drainage scheme, dugout for 126th Battery O.P. at C.19.a.8.8., emplacement for Heavy Trench Mortar Battery at B.12.d.3½.3½., excavating and revetting new trench from E.28, to junction of YORK and WHITE trench. Casualties 1 man gassed. Lieut. L. ROBSON rejoins company from BASE. Back Section. laying filter bed at COUTHOVE laundry, erection of bath house and ablution shed at PROVEN, fitting officers mess and building field kitchen in Camp "J".	
	14th		Sections on work as stated for August 13th. 11 Lieut G.H.GRAY rejoins company from hospital.	
	15th		Sections on works sames as stated for August 13th.	

AMcDerry, Major,
O/C 1st Durham Field Coy, R.E.

Army Form C. 2118.

WAR DIARY
or
INTELLIGENCE SUMMARY.   1/1st DURHAM FIELD COY. R.E.
(Erase heading not required.)

Instructions regarding War Diaries and Intelligence Summaries are contained in F.S. Regs., Part II. and the Staff Manual respectively. Title pages will be prepared in manuscript.

Place	Date	Hour	Summary of Events and Information	Remarks and references to Appendices
PESMILHOEK Camp A.20.b.8.8. and Canal Bank	1916 August 16th		Forward sections, dugouts in FARGATE at C.13.a.3.7., excavation for erection of elephantshelter at C.14.c.2.2., Medical Aid Post at C.13.a.3.7.5., deepening and widening, fitting "A" frames and trench boards.to FUSILIER trench at C.14.c.central., revetting STIRLING trench C.13.c.2.3., Patrolling and repairs to bridges., trench drainage scheme, emplacement for Heavy Trench Mortar Battery at B.12.d.9½.½, dugout for 126th Battery R.F.A,O.P.revetting new trench from E.28. Back section, laying filter bed at COUTHOVE laundry,, erecting bath house and ablution shed at PROVEN, erecting incinerator, fitting officers mess, and building field kitchen at "J" Camp	
	17th		------do------	
	18th		------do------	

AW Terry Major,
O/C 1st Durham Field Coy, R.E.

T2134. Wt. W708—776. 500000. 4/15. Sir J. C. & S.

Army Form C. 2118.

WAR DIARY
or
INTELLIGENCE SUMMARY. 1/1st DURHAM FIELD COY. R.E.
(Erase heading not required.)

Instructions regarding War Diaries and Intelligence Summaries are contained in F. S. Regs., Part II. and the Staff Manual respectively. Title pages will be prepared in manuscript.

Place	Date	Hour	Summary of Events and Information	Remarks and references to Appendices
PESELHOEK Camp. A.20.b.8.8.	1916. AUGUST. 19th		Forward sections, dugouts in FARGATE at C.13.a.3.7. Anglo-French bridge at B.12.d.8.7. new bridge at C.13.c.2.3. complete except steel shield, revetting STIRLING trench at C.14.c.d. trench and drainage scheme, dugout for 126th Battery R.F.A. O.P. at C.19.a.8.8. emplacement for Heavy Trench Mortar Battery at B.12.d.9½.½. revetting new trench from E.28. to YORK trench, Medical Aid Post, Deepening and widening FUSILIER trench C.14.c.central.	
CANAL BANK	20th		Back section work at GOUTHOVE laundry and R.E.Bark and camp fatigues. Sections on work as stated for 19th.	

(signature) Major,
O/C 1st Durham Field Coy, R.E.

T.134. W. W708-776. 500000. 4/15. Sir J.C. & S.

Army Form C. 2118.

WAR DIARY
or
INTELLIGENCE SUMMARY. 1/1st DURHAM FIELD COY, R.E.

(Erase heading not required.)

Instructions regarding War Diaries and Intelligence Summaries are contained in F. S. Regs., Part II. and the Staff Manual respectively. Title pages will be prepared in manuscript.

Place	Date	Hour	Summary of Events and Information	Remarks and references to Appendices.
PESELHOEK. A.20.b.8.8.	1916. AUGUST. 21st	9-45 p.m.	Nos. 2, 3, & 4 sections, (forward sections), moved from CANAL BANK to CAMP A.20.b.8.8. relieved by 124th Field Coy, R.E. Back section on work at GOUTHOVE laundry and Camp fatigues. Lieut. R.W. WILLIAMS admitted to 11th Field Ambulance.	
	22nd		Rest day, general inspections of arms equipment etc. 2 officers 10 other ranks moved from camp A.20.b.8.8. to POST OFFICE, YPRES to take over work from 7th Canadian Field Co. R.E. Draft of 4 men from No. 2 Territorial BASE, ROUEN.	
	23rd	7-30 p.m.	Headquarters, Nos 1, 3, & 4 sections moved from Camp A.20.b.8.8. to POST OFFICE, YPRES to billet, and for work in line.	
			Back section work on GOUTHOVE laundry and camp fatigues, and work in R.E. shops.	
POST OFFICE YPRES	24th		Back sections ----------do----------------do-----------do--------- Forward sections, night work, WELLINGTON CRESCENT trench, cutting traverses, building parapets, fitting "A" frames and excavating North end of trench.	

(signature) Major,
O/C 1st Durham Field Coy, R.E.

Army Form C. 2118.

WAR DIARY
or
INTELLIGENCE SUMMARY. 1/1st DURHAM FIELD COY. R.E.
(Erase heading not required.)

Instructions regarding War Diaries and Intelligence Summaries are contained in F.S. Regs, Part II. and the Staff Manual respectively. Title pages will be prepared in manuscript.

Place	Date	Hour	Summary of Events and Information	Remarks and references to Appendices
YPRES, and CAMP H.13.	1916. AUGUST.			
	25th.		Forward sections, night work on WELLINGTON CRESCENT trench, I.23.b. improving traverses, parapet and parados, preparing "A" frames for revetment, cleaning trench, and repairing tramway.	
	26th.		Back section and mounted section moved from Camp A.20.b.8.8. to Camp H.13.c. Forward sections on work as stated for 25th, night work. Back section camp fatigues.	
	27th.		Forward sections, night work, WELLINGTON CRESCENT trench, I.23½.b. improving traverses, parapet and parados, excavating and revetting trench, and cutting dugouts. VINCE trench, I.24.a., widening and clearing for communication. Back section work at COUTHOVE laundry, trench boards at R.E. Park.	
	28th.		Sections on work as stated for 27th.	
	29th.		Sections on work as stated for 27th.	
	30th.		Sections on work as stated for 27th.	
	31st		Forward sections, improving trench and revetting WELLINGTON CRESCENT, laying trench boards in VINCE trench. Lieut. R.W. WILLIAMS reported from hospital. Back section. work on COUTHOVE laundry, making "A" frames and trench boards in R.E. Park.	

CHW Major,
O/C 1st Durham Field Coy, R.E.

4th DIVISION.

1/1ST DURHAM FIELD COMPANY.

ROYAL ENGINEERS.

SEPTEMBER 1916.

WAR DIARY.

BY

THE OFFICER COMMANDING 1/1st DURHAM FIELD COY R. E.

FOR THE MONTH OF

SEPTEMBER 1916.

Army Form C. 2118.

WAR DIARY
or
INTELLIGENCE SUMMARY.   1/1st Durham Field Coy. R.E.
(Erase heading not required.)

Instructions regarding War Diaries and Intelligence Summaries are contained in F. S. Regs., Part II. and the Staff Manual respectively. Title pages will be prepared in manuscript.

Place	Date	Hour	Summary of Events and Information	Remarks and references to Appendices
POST OFFICE. YPRES. & CAMP PH.13.c.	1915 Sept. 1st		Headquarters and three sections billeted in POST OFFICE, YPRES, improving parapet and parados building traverses with sandbag revetment on WELLINGTON CRESCENT LIVING TRENCH, I.23.b. clearing and revetting VINCE TRENCH, laying trench boards RAMPARTS - ZILLEBEEKE BUND. One section billeted at H.13.c. on work at R.E. Park, and work at COUTMOVE laundry.	
	2nd.		Forward sections, cutting sleeping mined shelters, communications, clearing and improving trench for "A" frames at I.23.b. WELLINGTON CRESCENT. Laying trench boards RAMPARTS - ZILLEBEEKE. Back section on work at R.E. Park and COUTMOVE laundry.	
	3rd		------do------ clearing through and draining I.17.d. ROSSLYNN trench, improving drainage through front line I.18.a. SAVOY trench.	
	4th		------do------ ------do------ ------do------	
	5th		------do------ ------do------ ------do------	

J.B. Nall Major.
O/C 1st Durham Field Coy. R.E.

Army Form C. 2118.

WAR DIARY
or
INTELLIGENCE SUMMARY.
(Erase heading not required.)

1/1st Durham Field Coy., R.E.

Instructions regarding War Diaries and Intelligence Summaries are contained in F.S. Regs., Part II. and the Staff Manual respectively. Title pages will be prepared in manuscript.

Place	Date	Hour	Summary of Events and Information	Remarks and references to Appendices
POST OFFICE YPRES. & CAMP H.13.c.	1916. Sept. 6th.		Forward sections repairing revetting frames, laying trench boards, draing and clearing I.24.d VINCE trench, clearing trench, laying floor boards, building parapet, fixing "A" frames, and revetting I.23.b. WELLINGTON CRUSCENT, LIVING TRENCH. Revetting and repairing and laying trench boards I.24.d. VINCE TRENCH, draining and deepening I.18.a. SAVOY TRENCH. Laying trencg boards RAMPARTS - ZILLEBEKE. Back section work on COUTHOVE laundry, making trench boards at R.E. Park.	
	7th.		------do------	
	8th.		Headquarters, and Forward sections left POST OFFICE, YPRES, at 9-0 pm, Back section and mounted section left Camp H.13.c at 2-30 pm. Sections billeted as follows :-	
	9th.		Headquarters and No. 4 Section Camp A.15.b.9.5. PESELHOEK, No 1 section Camp A.28.Central, No. 2 Section Camp C.26.b.4.1. attached to C.R.E. 38th Division. No 3 Section ST.JAN-TER-BIEZEN.	

A B Hall Major.
O/C 1st Durham Field Coy. R.E.

Army Form C. 2118.

WAR DIARY
or
INTELLIGENCE SUMMARY.
(Erase heading not required.)

1/1st Durham Field Coy., R.E.

Instructions regarding War Diaries and Intelligence Summaries are contained in F.S. Regs., Part II. and the Staff Manual respectively. Title pages will be prepared in manuscript.

Place	Date	Hour	Summary of Events and Information	Remarks and references to Appendices
	1916.			
FESELMOKK CAMP A.15.b.9.5.	Sept. 10th.		Back sections :- Camp fatigues, cutting brush wood, making facines, preparing for the erection of horse-standings, erection of huts, latrines, building up and repairing roads. Forward Section:- preparing for the building of Machine Gun emplacement, cutting fire and communication trenches C.26.b.4.1. 1i Lieut. G.V. HURD attached to 2nd Army School of Instruction.	
	11th		------do------------do------------do------------do---	
	12th		------do------------do------------do------------do--- Draft of two men from No 2 Territorial Base, ROUEN.	
	13th		Same as stated for 10thSeptember.	
	14th		------do------do------do------	
	15th		------do------do------ Lieut. S. PEARSON struck off strength of Company.	

J.R.Bell Major,
O/C 1st Durham Field Coy, R.E.

Army Form C. 2118.

WAR DIARY
or
INTELLIGENCE SUMMARY. 1/1st Durham Field Coy, R.E.
(Erase heading not required.)

Instructions regarding War Diaries and Intelligence Summaries are contained in F. S. Regs., Part II. and the Staff Manual respectively. Title pages will be prepared in manuscript.

Place	Date	Hour	Summary of Events and Information	Remarks and references to Appendices
	1916.			
PESELHOEK CAMP A.15.b.9.5.	Sept. 16th.		Company detached from C.R.E. 38th Division. Left PESELHOEK, camp A.15.b.9.5. at 3-0 pm and proceeded to PROVEN.	
	17th.		Company entrained at PROVEN at 1-45 pm, for LONGPRE. Major J.B. Hall rejoins company from C.R.E. 4th Division.	
ALLONVILLE	18th		Company detrained at LONGPRE 2-30 am, and marched to ALLONVILLE arriving at 8-30 am. to billet. 2nd Lieut. G.V. Hurd rejoins company from 2nd Army School of Instruction.	
	19th.		Company drill and lectures on consolidation, of positions, and organization of working parties. 2nd Lieut F.F. CHAVERTON joined company from ENGLAND.	
	20th.		Same as stated for 19th.	
	21st		Same as stated for 19th.	
	22nd		Same as stated for 19th.	
	23rd.		Same as stated for 19th.	

J.B. Hall Major.
O/C 1st Durham Field Co. R.E.

Army Form C. 2118

WAR DIARY
or
INTELLIGENCE SUMMARY
(Erase heading not required.)

1/1st Durham Field Coy, R.E.

Instructions regarding War Diaries and Intelligence Summaries are contained in F.S. Regs., Part II and the Staff Manual respectively. Title Pages will be prepared in manuscript.

Place	Date	Hour	Summary of Events and Information	Remarks and references to Appendices
	1916.			
ALLONVILLE	Sept. 24th.		Company marched from ALLONVILLE to CORBIE.	
CORBIE	" 25th		Company moved from CORBIE to MERICOURT-L'ABBE.	
MERICOURT L'ABBE.	" 26th		Company moved from MERICOURT-L'ABBE to MEAULTE.	
MEAULTE	" 27th		Company moved from MEAULTE to CARNOY to Camp A.13.c.5.O. Major A.M.Terry handed over command of company to Major J.B. Hall, and then proceeded to 4th Division Headquarters.	
CARNOY.	" 28th		Company attached to Chief Engineer, XIV Corps, making lorry sidings.	
	" 29th		Making lorry sidings, completed 16.	
	" 30th.		Marking out sites for Battalion Camps.	

Shielded
Lieut
C.R.E. 4th Division

J.B.Hall Major.
O/C 1st Durham Field Coy, R.E.

4th DIVISION.

1/1ST DURHAM FIELD COMPANY.

ROYAL ENGINEERS.

OCTOBER 1916.

Army Form C. 2118.

WAR DIARY
or
INTELLIGENCE SUMMARY.   1/1st DURHAM FIELD COY. R.E.
(Erase heading not required.)

Instructions regarding War Diaries and Intelligence Summaries are contained in F. S. Regs., Part II. and the Staff Manual respectively. Title pages will be prepared in manuscript.

Place	Date	Hour	Summary of Events and Information	Remarks and references to Appendices
	1916. OCTOBER			
CARNOY	1st.		Company attached to Chief Engineer XIV Corps for work. Employed on making lorry sidings.	
CAMP	2nd		All sections employed on the making of lorry sidings. Lieut. T.R.WEIR rejoins from hospital.	
F.18.c. 5.9.	3rd		-----------do----------- 18 sidings completed.	
	4th		Selecting and preparing ground for the erection of Battalion Camp.	
	5th		Preparing ground for the erection of Battalion Camp. Lieut, L. ROBSON proceeded to hospital.	
	6th		-----------do----------- and erecting huts.	
	7th		-----------do----------- -----------do-----------	
	8th		Rest day, general inspection of arms, equipment, and church parade.	
	9th	9 am	Company moved from CARNOY to forward area S.24.b.9.5. near GINCHY relieving 1/1st EDINBURGH FIELD COY. R.E.	
	10th		Company attached to 12th Infantry Brigade. On general fatigues.	
GINCHY S.24.b. 9.5.	11th	12.5 am	Nos 1. 2. 3. & 4 sections moved from S.24.b.9.5. to T.8.Central.	
	12th		Sections await orders from 12th Infantry Brigade, for the consolidation of strong points during operation.	

J.R.Kell
Major.
O/C 1st Durham Field Coy, R.E.

Army Form C. 2118.

WAR DIARY
or
INTELLIGENCE SUMMARY.
(Erase heading not required.)

1/1st Durham Field Coy, R.E.

Instructions regarding War Diaries and Intelligence Summaries are contained in F. S. Regs., Part II. and the Staff Manual respectively. Title pages will be prepared in manuscript.

Place	Date	Hour	Summary of Events and Information	Remarks and references to Appendices
	1916			
GINCHY CAMP S.24.b.9.5.	13th		Making strong points at N.34.b.2.7 and N.34.b.3.5. mined dugouts at N.34.c.2.8. N.34.c.5.7. N.34.c.4.8. and T.8.Central. Repairs to Battalion Headquarters at N.34.c.1.9. Deepening and widening DONALD trench.	
	14th		------------do------------	
	15th		------------do------------	
	16th		Mining dugouts at N.34.c.2.8., N.34.c.5.7., N.34.c.4.8., N.34.b.2.7., N.34.b.3.5. Digging trench from RANGER to SPECTRUM, dugouts at T.8.Central.	
	17th		------------do------------	
			------------do------------	
			New trench from T.34.d.1.4 to T.34.d.4.1.,	
	18th		Same as stated for 17th.	
	19th		Communication trench from Ranger to Spectrum joined up, work on dugouts as above, Communication trench from WINDY to SUNKEN ROAD, and BERNAY. Lieut. G.H. GRAY admitted to hospital sick.	

[signature] Major,
O/C 1st Durham Field Coy, R.E.

Army Form C. 2118

WAR DIARY
or
INTELLIGENCE SUMMARY.

1/1st Durham Field Coy, R.E.

(Erase heading not required.)

Instructions regarding War Diaries and Intelligence Summaries are contained in F. S. Regs., Part II. and the Staff Manual respectively. Title pages will be prepared in manuscript.

Place	Date	Hour	Summary of Events and Information	Remarks and references to Appendices
	1916. October			
GINCHY S.24.b.9.5	20th		Communication trench from WINDY to BERNABY cut, communication from RANGER to SPECTRUM deepened and widened, mined dugouts at T.8.Central, N.34.c.2.8.	
	21st		Mined dugouts at T.8.Central and N.34.b.2.8.	
	22nd		------do------- new trench from T.4.b.3.8½ to T.4.b.1.e. 110yards long completed and occupied.	
			Casualties.Killed 1., wounded 8, shell shock 2.	
	23rd.		Mined dugouts at T.8.central and N.34.c.2.8.	
CITADEL	24th		Sections from T.8.Central rejoined company at S.24.b.9.5 and moved to CITADEL, relieved by 212th Field Coy, R.E.	
	25th		Rest day.	
	26th		Inspection of arms and equipment.	
MERICOURT	27th		Company moved from CITADEL to MERICOURT.	
	28th		Rest Day and general fatigues.	
	29th		Company entrained at MERICOURT at 2 pm for ALLERY, Mounted sections and transportby road.	

J.B.Mc?
Major.
O/C 1st Durham Field Co. R.E.

Army Form C. 2118

WAR DIARY
or
INTELLIGENCE SUMMARY.

1/1st Durham Field Coy, R.E.

(Erase heading not required.)

Instructions regarding War Diaries and Intelligence Summaries are contained in F. S. Regs., Part II. and the Staff Manual respectively. Title pages will be prepared in manuscript.

Place	Date	Hour	Summary of Events and Information	Remarks and references to Appendices
	1915			
ALLERY	30th		Detrained at AIRAINES and marched to ALLERY arrived 2-30 am.	
	31st		General fatigues, and inspection of arms and equipment.	

J.B.Stell Major,
O/C 1st Durham Field Coy, R.E.

4th DIVISION.

1/1ST DURHAM FIELD COMPANY.

ROYAL ENGINEERS.

NOVEMBER 1916.

Army Form C. 2118.

WAR DIARY
or
INTELLIGENCE SUMMARY

(Erase heading not required.)

1/1st Durham Field Coy., R.E.

Instructions regarding War Diaries and Intelligence Summaries are contained in F. S. Regs., Part II. and the Staff Manual respectively. Title pages will be prepared in manuscript.

Hour, Date, Place	Summary of Events and Information	Remarks and references to Appendices
BOUCHON November 1st 1915.	Company moved from ALLERY to BOUCHON, to be attached to Chief Engineer, 15th Corps for work.	
2nd	Selecting site and preparing for the erection of 15th Corps School of Instruction.	
3rd	Preparing ground for Range and erection of School.	
4th	---------do---------	
	Draft of 7 men from No. 2 Territorial Base.	
5th	Preparing ground for Range and erection of School.	
6th.	---------do---------	
	Lieut. T.H. WEIR rejoins Company from leave.	
7th	Preparing range and erection of school.	
8th	---------do---------	
9th	---------do---------	
10th	---------do---------	
	1 reinforcement from No. 2 Territorial Base.	

R. Black, Major.
O/C 1st Durham Field Coy, R.E.

Army Form C. 2118.

WAR DIARY
or
INTELLIGENCE SUMMARY 1/1st Durham Field Coy, R.E.
(Erase heading not required.)

Instructions regarding War Diaries and Intelligence Summaries are contained in F. S. Regs., Part II. and the Staff Manual respectively. Title pages will be prepared in manuscript.

Hour, Date, Place	Summary of Events and Information	Remarks and references to Appendices
BOUCHON 1915. November 11th.	Preparing range and erection of school. 2i Lieut. G.H. GRAY struck off company strength, evacuated to England, sick. 2i Lieut. J.S. BROWN proceeded to ENGLAND on leave.	
12th.	Preparing range and erection of school. Lieut. T.N. WEIR attached to No. 2 Company Train, 4th Division, for instruction in mounted duties.	
13th.	Preparing range and erection of school. 2i Lieut. A.J. STURINGS joined company from Base, and taken on the strength.	
14th	Erection of school.	
15th	-------do--------. Draft of 8 other ranks from No. 2 Territorial, Base and taken on strength.	

J.R. Hill Major,
O/C 1st Durham Field Coy, R.E.

Army Form C. 2118.

WAR DIARY
or
INTELLIGENCE SUMMARY. 1/1st Durham Field Coy, R.E.
(Erase heading not required.)

Instructions regarding War Diaries and Intelligence Summaries are contained in F.S. Regs. Part II and the Staff Manual respectively. Title pages will be prepared in manuscript.

Place	Date	Hour	Summary of Events and Information	Remarks and references to Appendices
	1916.			
BOUCHON	Nov. 16th		Company engaged on the erection of school.	
	17th		———do———	
	18th		———do——— Lieut. T.H. WEIR rejoins company.	
	19th		———do———	
	20th		———do———	
	21st		———do———	
	22nd		———do——— Draft of 5 other ranks from No. 2 Territorial Base taken on company strength.	

J.R. Hall Major.
O/C 1st Durham Field Coy, R.E.

Army Form C. 2118.

WAR DIARY
or
INTELLIGENCE SUMMARY.

1/1st Durham Field Coy, R.E.

(Erase heading not required.)

Instructions regarding War Diaries and Intelligence Summaries are contained in F. S. Regs. Part II. and the Staff Manual respectively. Title pages will be prepared in manuscript.

Place	Date	Hour	Summary of Events and Information	Remarks and references to Appendices
BURGHON	1916. November 23rd		Company engaged on the erection of 15th Corps School of Instruction. Major J.B. HALL proceeded to England on leave.	
	24th		Company engaged on the erection of School.	
	25th		--------do--------	
	26th		Rest Day. General Inspection of arms, equipment.	
	27th		Carrying on work, erection of School.	
	28th		--------do--------do--------	
	29th		--------do--------do--------	

J.W. Weir, Lieut.
O/C 1st Durham Field Coy, R.E.

Army Form C. 2118.

WAR DIARY
or
INTELLIGENCE SUMMARY.

(Erase heading not required.)

1/1st Durham Field Coy, R.E.

Instructions regarding War Diaries and Intelligence Summaries are contained in F. S. Regs., Part II. and the Staff Manual respectively. Title pages will be prepared in manuscript.

Place	Date	Hour	Summary of Events and Information	Remarks and references to Appendices
1918.				
BOUCHON	November 30th.		Erection of Corps School.	
			Work completed up to 30th November, 1918 :-	
			40 Nissen Huts completed. 27½' x 19'	
			1 Target store 18' x 15'	
			1 Magazine 50' x 15'	
			1 500 yard range with 32 target frames marking discs, and latrines.	
			2 Lecture huts 50' x 20'	
			1 Lecture hut 40' x 28' only 75 % completed.	
			2 Cookhouses 10' x 10'	
			1 Cookhouse 20' x 10'	
			3 Mess huts only 80% completed.	
			Targets and gun boxes.	

J H Owen, Lieut.
o/c 1st Durham Field Coy, R.E.

4th DIVISION.

1/1ST DURHAM FIELD COMPANY.

ROYAL ENGINEERS.

DECEMBER 1916.

Army Form C. 2118.

WAR DIARY
or
INTELLIGENCE SUMMARY.

(Erase heading not required.)

1/1st DURHAM FIELD CO. R.E.

Instructions regarding War Diaries and Intelligence Summaries are contained in F.S. Regs., Part II. and the Staff Manual respectively. Title pages will be prepared in manuscript.

Place	Date	Hour	Summary of Events and Information	Remarks and references to Appendices
BOUCHON	1916. DECEMBER 1st		General fatigues, preparing for move.	
	2nd		Dismounted sections moved from BOUCHON to FOUCAUCOURT. Lieut R.W. WILLIAMS proceeded on leave.	
FOUCAUCOURT	3rd		Dismounted sections on company training.	
	4th		---------do---------	
	5th		---------do---------	
	6th		---------do--------- Mounted section moved from BOUCHON to ARGOEUVES LONGPRE.	
	7th		Dismounted sections marched from FOUCAUCOURT to OISEMONT, entrained for MERICOURT, marched from MERICOURT to VAUX. Mounted section travelled by road from ARGOEUVES LONGPRE to VAUX.	
	8th		Company moved from VAUX to Camp 112 Major J.B. HALL rejoins company from leave.	

J.H. Deer Captain.
for O/C 1st Durham Field Coy. R.E.

Army Form C. 2118.

WAR DIARY
or
INTELLIGENCE SUMMARY.

1/1st Durham Field Coy, R.E.

(Erase heading not required.)

Instructions regarding War Diaries and Intelligence Summaries are contained in F.S. Regs., Part II. and the Staff Manual respectively. Title pages will be prepared in manuscript.

Place	Date	Hour	Summary of Events and Information	Remarks and references to Appendices
	1916. DECEMBER.			
CAMP 112	9th		Company moved from Camp 112 to Camp 16	
Camp 16	10th		General fatigues, rifle inspection, equipment etc.	
Camp 16 & MAURELAS RAVINE	11th		Nos 1 & 3 sections work in Camp 16, clearing light railway track and drainage. Nos 2 & 4 sections moved from Camp 16 to MAUREPAS RAVINE for work.	
	12th		No. 1 section overhauling and repairing Decauville track from Camp 16 to Camp 107. No. 3 Section moved from Camp 16 to MAUREPAS RAVINE. Nos 2 & 4 sections preparing dugouts for billets.	
	13th		No 1 Section overhauling Decauville track from Camp 16 to 107, drainage camp 16, moving horse-lines and erecting cover for same. Forward sections, making dugouts, relaying trench boards, repairing N.C.O.'s mess Divisional Headquarters.	
	14th		Sections on works as stated for 13th.	
	15th.		No 1 Section overhauling of Decauville track from Camp 16 to Camp 107 completed, and dump formed at each end, erecting horse standings and laying trench boards in camp 16. Forward sections, excavation of dugouts, wire fence to dugouts at Divisional Headquarters, drying shed at COMBLES, horse standings on MARICOURT - HARDECOURT road.	

J.W.Weir, Capt.
Major.
for O/C 1st Durham Field Coy, R.E.

Army Form C. 2118.

WAR DIARY
or
INTELLIGENCE SUMMARY.   1/1st DURHAM FIELD COY. R.E.
(Erase heading not required.)

Instructions regarding War Diaries and Intelligence Summaries are contained in F.S. Regs., Part II. and the Staff Manual respectively. Title Pages will be prepared in manuscript.

Place	Date	Hour	Summary of Events and Information	Remarks and references to Appendices
CAMP 16. & MAUREPAS RAVINE	1916. DECEMBER. 16th		No. 1 Section. Preparing billet for laundry at BRAY, horse standings, latrines, laying trench boards, drainage in Camp 16. Drainage camp 107. Preparing horse standings on MARICOURT - HARDECOURT road, drying shed at COMBLES. Excavation of site completed for workshops, and dugouts.	
	17th.		No 1 section. and forward sections as stated for 16th. Lieut. R.W. WILLIAMS rejoined company from leave. 2l Lieut. G.V. HURD proceeded on leave.	
	18th		No 1 section. Horse standings, laying trench boards, drainage, erecting latrines Camp 16. XXXXXXXXXXXXXXX Laying trench boards, drainage Camp 107, drying rooms BRONFAY FARM, drying for laundry at BRAY. Horse standings MARICOURT - HARDECOURT road, workshop in MAUREPAS RAVINE forward sections. completed, and dugouts.	
	19th		Same as stated for 18th.	

for O/C 1st Durham Field Coy, R.E.

Army Form C. 2118.

WAR DIARY
or
INTELLIGENCE SUMMARY.   1/1st DURHAM FIELD COY. R.E.

(Erase heading not required.)

Instructions regarding War Diaries and Intelligence Summaries are contained in F.S. Regs., Part II. and the Staff Manual respectively. Title pages will be prepared in manuscript.

Place	Date	Hour	Summary of Events and Information	Remarks and references to Appendices
Camp 16 and MAUREPAS RAVINE.	1916. DECEMBER 20th		No 1 Section. Completed drainage, relaying trench boards, erecting latrines Camp 16. Drainage, relaying trench boards, erecting latrines Camp 107. Drying rooms BRONFAY FARM, drying room for laundry at BRAY. Horse standings MARICOURT - HARDECOURT, dugouts, drying rooms at COMBLES. Forward sections. Reinforcements of 20 other ranks from No. 2 Territorial, Base taken on company strength.	
	21st		Same as stated for 20th.	
	22nd		Same as stated for 20th.	
	23rd		Same as stated for 20th.	
	24th		No 1 Section. Rest day. General inspection of arms, equipment, etc., Forward sections. Horse standings MARICOURT - HARDECOURT road, dugouts, machine-gun mountings fixed in position.	
	25th		Same as stated for 24th.	
	~~26th~~		~~Same as stated for 24th.~~ ~~1 Lieut. proceeded on leave.~~	

O/C 1st Durham Field Coy, R.E.

Army Form C. 2118.

WAR DIARY
or
INTELLIGENCE SUMMARY.

(Erase heading not required.)

1/1st DURHAM FIELD COY. R.E.

Instructions regarding War Diaries and Intelligence Summaries are contained in F.S. Regs., Part II. and the Staff Manual respectively. Title pages will be prepared in manuscript.

Place	Date	Hour	Summary of Events and Information	Remarks and references to Appendices
CAMP 16.	1916. DECEMBER 26th.		No. 1 Section. Drying rooms BRONFAY FARM, Divisional Baths BRONFAY FARM, relaying trench boards Camp 16, erecting incinerators, relaying and draining trench boards camp 107. Forward sections as stated for 24th. 2nd Lieut. W.P. CALVERTON proceeded on leave.	
	27th.		No. 1 Section. Divisional baths and drying room BRONFAY FARM, relaying trench boards, Camp 16, and 107, repairs to huts Camp 16. Nos 2. 3. & 4 Sections moved from MAUREPAS RAVINE to Camp 16.	
	28th.		Company moved from Camp 16 to SAILLY-LE-SEC.	
	29th.		General fatigues.	
	30th.		Rifle inspection, and company training.	
	31st		Company training.	

[signature] Capt.
[signature] O/C 1st Durham Field Coy, R.E.

4th Division
War Diaries
526th Field Coy, R.E, LATE
1/1 Durham

January to December
1917

Feb. 1919

4 DIVISION. TROOPS.
406 FIELD COY R.E.
(FORMERELY 1/1 RENFREW)
1916 APR TO 1919 JUNE.
526 FIELD COY R.E.
(FORMERELY 1/1 DURHAM)
1915 SEPT TO 1919 FEB.

WAR DIARY.

OF

526

The Officer Commanding the 1/1st Durham Field Coy. R.E.

FOR

JANUARY. 1917.

Army Form C. 2118.

WAR DIARY
or
INTELLIGENCE SUMMARY.   1/1st DURHAM FIELD COY. R.E.

(Erase heading not required.)

Instructions regarding War Diaries and Intelligence Summaries are contained in F.S. Regs. Part II. and the Staff Manual respectively. Title pages will be prepared in manuscript.

Place	Date	Hour	Summary of Events and Information	Remarks and references to Appendices
SAILLY-LE-SEC.	1917. JANUARY 1st		Part sections on works, constructing baths in Adrian hut at SAILLY-LAURETTE, drying rooms, and ironing rooms. Making beds for 14th Infantry Brigade, repairs to billets at SAILLY-LE-SEC, instructional trench and dugout at Camp 12, anti-gas hut for 4th Division gas school. Remainder of company, drill and company training.	
	2nd.		Same as stated for 1st.	
	3rd.		Same as stated for 1st.	
	4th.		Same as stated for 1st.	
	5th.		Constructing baths, drying room, ironing room at SAILLY-LAURETTE, beds for 12th Infantry Brigade, latrines for SAILLY-LE-SEC, repairs to billets and making signs boards for Town Major SAILLY-LE-SEC.	
	6th.		Carrying on work as above.	
	7th.		Carrying on work as above.	
	8th.		Carrying on work as above.	
	9th.		Carrying on work as above.	

for O/C 1st Durham Field Coy, R.E.

Captain.

Army Form C 2118.

WAR DIARY
or
INTELLIGENCE SUMMARY.

1/1st DURHAM FIELD COY. R.E.

(Erase heading not required.)

Instructions regarding War Diaries and Intelligence Summaries are contained in F.S. Regs., Part II. and the Staff Manual respectively. Title pages will be prepared in manuscript.

Place	Date	Hour	Summary of Events and Information	Remarks and references to Appendices
SAILLY-LE-SEC.	1917. JANUARY 10th.		Sections on work as follows :- Constructing baths at SAILLY-LAURETTE, beds for 12th Infantry Brigade, repairs to billets at SAILLY-LE-SEC, instructional trench and dugout at camp 12. Lieut. G.R.M. BRACKENREG joined company.	
	11th.		Carrying on work as above.	
	12th.		Carrying on work as above.	
	13th.		Carrying on work as above.	
	14th.		Rest Day.	
	15th.		Carrying on work as stated for 10th.	
	16th.		Company moved from SAILLY-LE-SEC to SUZANNE.	
SUZANNE	17th.		Company moved from SUZANNE. Headquarters and Mounted Section to CURLU area A.29.b. Nos 1. 2. 3. and 4 Sections to B.30.b.	
CURLU.	18th.		Sections on work improving dugouts and erecting latrines.	
	19th.		Sections on work constructing mined dugouts at C.20.d.2.9., improving approaches to GARNIER CASTENAL trenches, water supply at B.30.c.5.5. Reinforcements from Base, 2 N.C.O's and Sapper.	

J.W.Weir capt.
for O/C 1st Durham Field Co. R.E.

Army Form C. 2118.

WAR DIARY
or
INTELLIGENCE SUMMARY.   1/1st DURHAM FIELD COY? R.E.
(Erase heading not required.)

Instructions regarding War Diaries and Intelligence Summaries are contained in F. S. Regs., Part II. and the Staff Manual respectively. Title pages will be prepared in manuscript.

Place	Date	Hour	Summary of Events and Information	Remarks and references to Appendices
CURLU.	1917. JANUARY. 20th		Sections on work, improving communication trenches GASTINEL and GARNIER (C.20.d.2.9.) mined dugouts at C.20.d.2.9. working water supply and completing latrines at B.30.c.5.5. Casualty. No. 1785 Sapper DODDS J. killed in action by shell fire.	
	21st		Carrying on work as stated for 20th.	
	22nd.		Nos. 1. 2. 3. and 4 Sections moved from B.30.b. to A.29.b.	

Weir, Captain,
for O/C 1st Durham Field Coy, R.E.

Army Form C. 2118.

WAR DIARY
or
INTELLIGENCE SUMMARY. 1/1st DURHAM FIELD COY. R.E.

(Erase heading not required.)

Instructions regarding War Diaries and Intelligence Summaries are contained in F. S. Regs., Part II. and the Staff Manual respectively. Title pages will be prepared in manuscript.

Place	Date	Hour	Summary of Events and Information	Remarks and references to Appendices
CURLU A.29.b	1917. January 23rd		Company moved from CURLU area, No 1 Section to Camp 18 G.10.c.7.3. Remainder of company to F.c.6. (L.18.a).	
SUZANNE L.18.a.	24th.		No 1 Section Camp 18. erecting latrines and incinerators, repairing beds in Adrien huts. Remainder of company Camp F.c.6. cleaning and repairing quarters, erecting cookhouses, latrines.	
	25th.		No. 1 Section Camp 18 Remainder F.C.6., carrying on work as stated for 24th.	
	26th.		No 1 Section Camp 18., erecting latrines, incinerators, water supply and repairing beds. Remainder of company, constructing drying room for gum-boots at SUZANNE, dugout for R.H.A. at G.9.central (ALBERT MAP). general work in Camp F.c.6. constructing laundry and drying room at G.8.d.	
	27th.		Sections as stated for 26th.	
	28th.		No 1 Section Camp 18., erection of latrines completed, repairs to pathways, water supply, and repairing beds. Remainder of company, drying room for gum-boots in SUZANNE, dugout for R.H.A. at G.9.central, laundry at G.9.8, erecting screens and covering horsestandings for A.S.C. at Camp 111.	
	29th.		------do------	
	30th.		------do------	
	31st.		------do------	

Wilson Capt.
For O/C 1st Durham Field Co. R.E.

W A R   D I A R Y

BY

THE OFFICER COMMANDING 526th (DURHAM) FIELD COMPANY R.E. (T)

FOR THE MONTH OF

FEBRUARY   1917.

Army Form C.2118.

WAR DIARY
or
INTELLIGENCE SUMMARY. 526th (Durham) Field Coy. R.E.

(Erase heading not required.)

Instructions regarding War Diaries and Intelligence Summaries are contained in F. S. Regs. Part II. and the Staff Manual respectively. Title pages will be prepared in manuscript.

Place	Date	Hour	Summary of Events and Information	Remarks and references to Appendices
SUZANNE Camp P.c.6. (L.18.a.).	1917. FEBRUARY 1st		No 1 Section Camp 18 erecting cookhouses and latrines, preparing Divisional Canteen, improving Camp quarters and repairing beds. Headquarters and remainder of Company at camp P.c.6., repairing company stables, building stables for R.H.A. at G.9.central, erecting laundry for 4th Division at SUZANNE. Designation of company changed from 1/1st DURHAM FIELD CO. R.E. to 526th (DURHAM) FIELD CO. R.E.	
	2nd		Sections carrying on work as above.	
	3rd		Sections carrying on work as above.	
	4th		Sections carrying on work as above.	
	5th.		No. 1 Section Camp 18., erecting cookhouses and latrines, and improving billets, laying trench boards. Remainder of sections Repairs to company stables completed, preparing rooms for drying gum boots in SUZANNE, building stables for R.H.A. at G.9.d.5.2. erecting elephant for R.H.A., construction of laundry at SUZANNE, erecting screens, roofing stables, and erecting hut for A.S.C. at Camp 111.	
	6th.		Sections carrying on work as stated above. No 3 Section moved from Camp P.c.6., (L.18.a.) to B.30.b. to be attached to 406th (RENFREW) Field Co. R.E. for work.	

J.M.... Capt.
for O/C 526th (Durham) Field Co. R.E.

WAR DIARY
or
INTELLIGENCE SUMMARY.

526th (Durham) Field Co. R.E.

Army Form C.2118.

(Erase heading not required.)

Instructions regarding War Diaries and Intelligence Summaries are contained in F.S. Regs., Part II and the Staff Manual respectively. Title pages will be prepared in manuscript.

Place	Date	Hour	Summary of Events and Information	Remarks and references to Appendices
SUZANNE Camp P.C.6. (L.18.a.)	1917. 7th		No 1 Section, Camp 18., erection of cookhouses completed, erecting ablution shed, laying trench boards, building "Warwick" oven, assisting with water supply. Nos. 2 & 4 Sections, preparing road for A.S.C. Camp 111, erecting Calais shelter for R.H.A., erecting cookhouses and dump for A.S.C. camp 112.	
	8th		Rest day, inspections of arms, equipment, and smoke helmets.	
	9th		Carrying on work as stated for 7th.	
	10th		Carrying on work as stated for 7th.	
	11th		No 1 Section, camp 18., erecting ablution shed, cookhouse for Trench Mortar Battery Officers, erecting partitions in officers huts, and laying trench boards. Nos. 2 & 4 Sections., erecting Calais shelter for R.H.A., building ovens and erecting dump for A.S.C. camp 112, repairing stables and horsestandings camp P.c.6.	
	12th		Carrying on work as above.	
	13th		Carrying on work as above. Major J.B.HALL rejoined company from Senior Officers School of Instruction.	

J. Wells Capt.

for O/C 526th (Durham) Field Coy, R.E.

Army Form C. 2118.

WAR DIARY
or
INTELLIGENCE SUMMARY.

526th (Durham) Field Co. R.E.

(Erase heading not required.)

Instructions regarding War Diaries and Intelligence Summaries are contained in F. S. Regs., Part II. and the Staff Manual respectively. Title pages will be prepared in manuscript.

Place	Date	Hour	Summary of Events and Information	Remarks and references to Appendices
SUZANNE Camp P.c.6. (L.18.a.)	FEBRUARY 14th		No 1 Section Camp 18, erecting ablution shed, completed, erecting "Warwick" oven, laying trench boards, preparing for the erection of drying room. Nos 2 & 4 Sections, constructing laundry for 4th Division in SUZANNE, erecting field ovens for A.S.C. in camp 112, erecting dump for A.S.C. in camp 111, repairing to stables and horse standings in camp P.c.6.	
	15th.		Carrying on work as stated for 14th.	
	16th		Carrying on work as stated for 14th.	
	17th		Carrying on work as stated for 14th.	
	18th		Rest day, inspections of arms and equipment.	
	19th		Preparing for move, loading of vehicles and general fatigues. No 1 Section moved from Camp 18 to Camp P.c.6. (L.18.a.)	
	20th		Headquarters, Nos 1, 2 & 4 Section moved from Camp P.c.6, No. 3 Section from B.30.b, to camp 117. Draft of 7 men from No. 2 Territorial Base.	

J.A.West Capt.
for O/C 526th (Durham) Field Co. R.E.

Army Form C. 2118.

WAR DIARY
or
INTELLIGENCE SUMMARY.   526th (Durham) Field Co. R.E.

(Erase heading not required.)

Instructions regarding War Diaries and Intelligence Summaries are contained in F.S. Regs. Part II. and the Staff Manual respectively. Title pages will be prepared in manuscript.

Place	Date	Hour	Summary of Events and Information	Remarks and references to Appendices
	1917. February			
Camp 117	21st		Company moved from Camp 117 to CORBIE to billet.	
CORBIE	22nd		Arranging billets, inspection of arms, equipment, and smoke helmets.	
	23rd		Sections on company training, drill, and inspections, lectures by section officers.	
	24th		---------do---------	
	25th		---------do--------- and Church parade.	
	26th		Sections on company training, drill, inspections, and lectures by sections officers.	
	27th		---------do---------	
	28th		---------do---------	

J.W.W. Capt.
for O/C 526th (Durham) Field Co. R.E.

WAR   DIARY

BY

THE OFFICER COMMANDING 526th (DURHAM) FIELD COMPANY. R. E.

FOR THE MONTH OF

MARCH 1917.

Army Form C. 2118.

WAR DIARY
or
INTELLIGENCE SUMMARY. 526th (Durham) Field Co. R.E.

(Erase heading not required.)

Instructions regarding War Diaries and Intelligence Summaries are contained in F.S. Regs., Part II. and the Staff Manual respectively. Title pages will be prepared in manuscript.

Place	Date	Hour	Summary of Events and Information	Remarks and references to Appendices
	March 1917.			
CORBIE.	1st		Section and Company drill, cleaning transport, lectures on Map reading and Instruments, rifle exercises and route march.	
	2nd.		------do------	
	3rd.		Company moved from CORBIE to ST. GRATIEN.	
ST. GRATIEN.	4th.		Company moved from ST. GRATIEN to LAVICOGNE.	
LAVIC- OGNE.	5th.		Company moved from LAVICOGNE to GEZAINCOURT.	
GEZAIN- COURT.	6th.		Company moved from GEZAINCOURT to SERICOURT,	
SERICOURT	7th.		Company moved from SERICOURT to SAVY.	
SAVY	8th.		Company moved from SAVY to BRAY near ARRAS, relieving 20th Field Coy. R.E. and attached to C.E. 17th Corps for work.	
BRAY	9th.		Sections on work as follows :- completing ammunition dumps, erecting Nissen huts.	
	10th		------do------	
	11th		Rest Day. Inspection of arms, equipment, smoke helmets etc..	

for O/C 526th (Durham) Field Coy. R.E.

Army Form C. 2118.

WAR DIARY
or
INTELLIGENCE SUMMARY.   526th (Durham) Field Coy. R.E.
(Erase heading not required.)

Instructions regarding War Diaries and Intelligence Summaries are contained in F.S. Regs., Part II. and the Staff Manual respectively. Title pages will be prepared in manuscript.

Place	Date	Hour	Summary of Events and Information	Remarks and references to Appendices
BRAY.	1917 March 12th.		Sections on works, ammunition dump BRAY, erecting Nissen huts at No. 5 Camp X Hutments F.19.a.	
	13th.		Carrying on work as above.	
	14th.		Carrying on work as above.	
	15th.		Carrying on work as above.	
	16th.		Carrying on work as above.	
	17th.		Carrying on work as above.	
	18th.		Rest day, inspections of arms, equipment, P.H. Helmets, Box respirators, etc., Church parade.	
	19th.		Sections on work, ammunition dump at MAROEUIL, ammunition dump at BRAY completed, erecting Nissen huts at No. 5 Camp X Hutments F.19.a. and BOIS de MAROEUIL F.21.c.3.	
	20th.		Carrying on work as above.	
	21st.		Carrying on work as above.	
	22nd.		Carrying on work as above.	
	23rd.		Carrying on work as above.	
	24th.		Carrying on work as above.	

[signature] Capt., R.E.
for O/C 526th (Durham) Field Coy. R.E.

Army Form C. 2118.

WAR DIARY
or
INTELLIGENCE SUMMARY. 526th (Durham) Field Co. R.E.

(Erase heading not required.)

Place	Date	Hour	Summary of Events and Information	Remarks and references to Appendices
BRAY.	1917. March 25th		Rest day, inspections of arms, equipment, and church parade.	
	26th		Sections on making ammunition dump MAROEUIL, erecting Nissen huts at BOIS de MAROEUIL, making ramps, rebuilding bridges, cutting latrines etc, for 4th Division assembly grounds at 6,a.4.c.4, 6,c.4,c.6, excavation for loop road way at BRAY, blinds for ammunition dump at BRAY.	
	27th		Carrying on work as above.	
	28th		Carrying on work as above.	
	29th		Carrying on work as above.	
	30th		Carrying on work as above.	
	31st		Carrying on work as above. Work completed :- ammunition dump at MAROEUIL 90%, loop road way at BRAY, completed, blinds for ammunition dump 90% completed, 1 hut for Household Battalion Headquarters, 1 Hut for 86th Battery R.F.A. Wagon Lines.	

[signature] Capt.

for O/C 526th (Durham) Field Coy. R.E.

WAR   DIARY

BY

THE OFFICER COMMANDING 526th (DURHAM) FIELD COMPANY R.E.

FOR MONTH OF APRIL 1917.

526th (DURHAM) FIELD COY. R.E.

Army Form C. 2118.

WAR DIARY
or
INTELLIGENCE SUMMARY.

(Erase heading not required.)

Place	Date	Hour	Summary of Events and Information	Remarks and references to Appendices
BRAY	1917. APRIL 1st.		Rest day, inspections of arms, equipment, etc.	
Near ARRAS	2nd.		No 3 Section preparing assembly ground for 11th Infantry Brigade. G.8.d. G.14.b. Sections on work, erection of Nissen huts and ammunition dump at MAROEUIL. Preparing assembly ground at G.8.d. and G.14.b.	
	3rd.		Carrying on work as above.	
	4th.		Carrying on work as above.	
	5th.		Carrying on work as above.	
	6th.		Carrying on work as above.	
	7th.		Carrying on work as above. Company under orders of G.O.C. 11th Infantry Brigade from 7 p.m.	
	8th.		Rest day, inspections of arms, equipment, etc.	

Miller Capt.
for O/C 526th (Durham) Field Co. R.E.

Army Form C. 2118.

526th (DURHAM) FIELD COY. R.E.

WAR DIARY
or
INTELLIGENCE SUMMARY.
(Erase heading not required.)

Instructions regarding War Diaries and Intelligence Summaries are contained in F. S. Regs., Part II. and the Staff Manual respectively. Title pages will be prepared in manuscript.

Place	Date	Hour	Summary of Events and Information	Remarks and references to Appendices
BRAY. near ARRAS.	1917. APRIL. 9th.	6-30 am.	Headquarters and dismounted sections moved from BRAY to assembly ground G.8.d. thence to H.7.d.central, attached to 11th Infantry Brigade for movement orders during operation. Lieut. G.R.M. BRACKENREG slightly wounded by shell fire. 1 other rank wounded by shell fire admitted to hospital.	
		8.pm.	Nos 1 and 2 Sections proceeded to H.10.a.3.5., H.10.d.4.8., H.11.c.1.3., H.11.c.8.5. for the making of strong points. No. 4 Section repairing and opening out roads from H.7.d.9.0., to H.9.a.2.7., and from H.13.b.9.3., to H.15.a.1.0.	
H.7.d. central.	10th.	8.p.m.	Completing strong points and carrying on work of repairing roads.	
FAMPOUX	11th.		Headquarters and dismounted sections moved from H.7.d.central to FAMPOUX. Carrying on work of repairing roads.	
H.7.d. central.	12th.		Headquarters and dismounted sections moved from FAMPOUX to H.7.d.central. Mounted section moved from BRAY to G.17.c.1.3.Lieut. G.R.M. BRACKENREG transferred to No. 7 Tramway Company 5th Army. Struck off strength.	
	13th.		Sections working on road repairs.	
	14th.		---------do---------- Mounted section moved from G.17.c.1.3 to G.9.c.8.2.	
	15th.		Sections working on road repairs.	
	16th.		Sections on road repairs.	
	17th.		Sections on road repairs. Casualties 1 N.C.O. killed by shell fire.	

for O/c 526th (Durham) Field Co. R.E.
[signature] Capt.

Army Form C. 2118.

WAR DIARY
or
INTELLIGENCE SUMMARY.
(Erase heading not required.)

5¬oth (DURHAM) FIELD COY. R.E.

Instructions regarding War Diaries and Intelligence Summaries are contained in F. S. Regs., Part II. and the Staff Manual respectively. Title pages will be prepared in manuscript.

Place	Date	Hour	Summary of Events and Information	Remarks and references to Appendices
H.7.d. central.	1917. APRIL. 18th.		Sections on road repairs.	
	19th.		Sections on road repairs. Mounted section moved from G.9.c.8.2., to G.16.a.7.9.	
LARASSET	20th.		Headquarters and dismounted sections moved from H.7.d. central, mounted section from G.16.a.7.9. to LARASSET.	
IZEL-LES-HAMEAU.	21st.		Company moved from LARASSET to IZEL-LES-HAMEAU.	
	22nd.		Rest day - inspections of arms, equipment and Church parade. 5 other ranks reinforcements from No. 5 Reinforcement Company taken on strength.	
	23rd.		Sections on training :- drill and physical exercises.	
	24th.		------do------------do------------do-----------	
	25th.		------do------------do------------do-----------	
			Lecture by C.R.E. 4th Division to Officers and N.C.O's on strong points consolidation.	
	26th.		Sections laying out and digging strong points for instructional purpose.	
	27th.		Drill and physical exercises, instruction on strong points.	
	28th.		Company moved from IZEL-LES-HAMEAU to FREVIN-CAPELLE.	
	29th.		Company moved from Frevin-Capelle to "Y" Hutments.	
	30th.		Company moved from "Y" Hutments, dismounted sections to G.18.c., mounted section to G.16.b.3.5.	

J.M.W. Capt.
O/C 5¬oth (Durham) Field Coy R.E.

WAR   DIARY

BY

THE OFFICER COMMANDING 526th (DURHAM) FIELD COY. R.E.

FOR MONTH OF

MAY 1917.

Army Form C. 2118.

WAR DIARY
or
INTELLIGENCE SUMMARY.

(Erase heading not required.)

526th (Durham) Field Co. R.E.

Instructions regarding War Diaries and Intelligence Summaries are contained in F.S. Regs., Part II. and the Staff Manual respectively. Title pages will be prepared in manuscript.

REFERENCE MAPS :- TRENCH MAP, ARRAS 51B.N.W.3. EDITION 7.A. 1/10,000.
TRENCH MAP, FAMPOUX, 51 B.N.W.4. EDITION 3.A. 1/10,000.

Place	Date	Hour	Summary of Events and Information	Remarks and references to Appendices
ST. NICHOLAS.	1917. May 1st.		Sections on work, repairing ATHIES - FAMPOUX road, transporting pontoons from ANZIN to ATHIES LOCK, improving accomodation for Divisional Headquarters in Railway cutting at H.13.b.o.7.	
	2nd.		Carrying on repairs to ATHIES - FAMPOUX road, collecting pontoons on RIVER SCARPE, and work on Divisional Headquarters.	
	3rd.		Constructing strong point at H.18.d.8.4., navigating pontoons with wounded from FAMPOUX to ATHIES LOCK. (night work). Casualties, 2 Lieut. J.S. BROWN and 2 other ranks wounded.	
	4th.		Completing strong point at H.18.d.8.4., wiring EFFIE TRENCH, constructing dugout for 11th Infantry Brigade Headquarters at H.16.d.2.8. (Day and night work).	
	5th.		Carrying on work on dugout for 11th Infantry Brigade Headquarters, and improving Divisional Headquarters. 2/Lieut. J.S. BROWN struck off strength.	
	6th.		Wiring EFFIE TRENCH, 11th Infantry Brigade dugout, and work on Divisional Headquarters.	
	7th.		Wiring PIKE and EFFIE TRENCHES, dugout for 11th Infantry Brigade, day and night work work on or Divisional Headquarters.	
	8th.		Wiring PIKE TRENCH, regimental aid post under Railway Bridge H.24.a.4.8., work on dugout for 11th Infantry Brigade and Divisional Headquarters.	

Owen Capt.
for O/C 526th (Durham) Field Co. R.E.

Army Form C.2118.

WAR DIARY
or
INTELLIGENCE SUMMARY. 526th (Durham) Field Co. R.E
(Erase heading not required.)

Instructions regarding War Diaries and Intelligence Summaries are contained in F. S. Regs., Part II. and the Staff Manual respectively. Title pages will be prepared in manuscript.

Place	Date	Hour	Summary of Events and Information	Remarks and references to Appendices
St. NICOLAS.	1917. May 9th.		Work on Regimental Aid Post at H.24.a.5.8., wiring PIKE TRENCH, work on Divisional Headquarters accomodation, and dugout for 11th Infantry Brigade Headquarters.	
	10th.		Completing dugout for 11th Infantry Brigade Headquarters, work on Divisional Headquarters accomodation. One section resting. One section assembled in CRUMP TRENCH at midnight for work following day.	
	11th.		Construction of Machine Gun emplacements, in Railway embankment about I.13.b.9.2. Navigating pontoons for the evacuation of wounded from FAMPOUX to ATHIES LOCK.	
	12th.		Carrying on work as for 11th. Casualties, 1 other rank, killed, 5 other ranks wounded.	
	13th.		Forward Sections moved from BLANGY (G.18.c.35.60.) to ARRAS. Attached to Chief Engineer, 17th Corps for work.	
	14th.		Sections making road, BLANGY, from G.24.a.4.6., to G.24.a.65.90.	
	15th.		Carrying on work on road.	
	16th.		Carrying on work on road.	

L.W.Weir Capt.
for O/C 526th (Durham) Field Co. R.E.

Army Form C. 2118.

WAR DIARY
or
~~INTELLIGENCE SUMMARY~~ 526th (Durham) Field Co R.E.

(Erase heading not required.)

Instructions regarding War Diaries and Intelligence Summaries are contained in F.S. Regs., Part II. and the Staff Manual respectively. Title pages will be prepared in manuscript.

Place	Date	Hour	Summary of Events and Information	Remarks and references to Appendices
ARRAS.	1917. May 17th.		Making road, BLANGY, from G.24.a.4.6. to G.24.a.65.90.	
	18th.		Carrying on work as above.	
	19th.		Carrying on work as above.	
	20th.		Carrying on work as above. Wiring Corps Line from H.9.a.2.8., to H.22.a. (night work).	
	21st.		Carrying on work as above.	
	22nd.		Carrying on work as above.	
	23rd.		Carrying on work as above.	
	24th.		Carrying on work as above.	
	25th.		Carrying on work as above.	
	26th.		Carrying on work as above. 10 other ranks reinforcements from No. 6 R.E. Reinforcement Co.	
	27th.		Rest day. Inspections of arms, equipment, etc.	

J. Weh Capt.
for O/C 526th (Durham) Field Co. R.E.

Army Form C. 2118.

WAR DIARY
or
~~INTELLIGENCE SUMMARY~~ 526th (Durham) Field Co. R.E

(Erase heading not required.)

Instructions regarding War Diaries and Intelligence Summaries are contained in F. S. Regs., Part II. and the Staff Manual respectively. Title pages will be prepared in manuscript.

Place	Date	Hour	Summary of Events and Information	Remarks and references to Appendices
ARRAS.	1917. May.			
	28th.		Carrying on work on road making. Wiring of Corps Line completed.	
	29th.		Carrying on work on road making.	
	30th.		Carrying on work on road making.	
	31st.		Company Moved : Dismounted sections from ARRAS, mounted section and transport from G.16.b.3.5. to TILLOY-LES-HERMAVILLE, to work under orders of G.R.E. 4th Division.	

[signature] Capt.

for O/c 526th (Durham) Field Co. R.E.

WAR   DIARY

BY

THE OFFICER COMMANDING 526th (DURHAM) FIELD CO. R.E.

FOR MONTH OF

JUNE 1917.

Army Form C. 2118.

WAR DIARY
or
INTELLIGENCE SUMMARY.

526th (Durham) Field Co. R.E.

(Erase heading not required.)

Place	Date	Hour	Summary of Events and Information	Remarks and references to Appendices
TILLOY-LES-HERMAVILLE.	1917. JUNE 1st.		Rest day. Inspections of arms, equipment, and gas appliances. Major J.B. HALL proceeded to England on leave.	
	2nd.		2 N.C.O's and 6 Sappers attached to each Battalion of the 12th Infantry Brigade, to instruct on the following subjects:- wiring, tracing and laying out of fire and communication trenches and strong points, correct use of the pick and shovel, instruction given both day and night. Battalions instructed, Duke of Wellingtons Regiment, Lancashire Fusiliers, Essex Regiment, and King's Own Regiment. Remainder of company on drill, and company training.	
	3rd.		Carrying on work as above.	
	4th.		Carrying on work as above.	
	5th.		Carrying on work as above. 2/Lieut. H. HINKS joined company from England. 3 other ranks from Base.	
	6th.		Carrying on work as above.	
	7th.		Carrying on work as above.	

J.W. Webb Capt.
for o/c 526th (Durham) Field Co. R.E.

Army Form C. 2118.

WAR DIARY
or
INTELLIGENCE SUMMARY

526th (Durham) Field Co. R.E.

(Erase heading not required.)

Instructions regarding War Diaries and Intelligence Summaries are contained in F. S. Regs., Part II. and the Staff Manual respectively. Title pages will be prepared in manuscript.

Place	Date	Hour	Summary of Events and Information	Remarks and references to Appendices
TILLOY-LES-HERMAVILLE.	1917. JUNE 8th.		MAP REFERENCE:- TRENCH MAP, FRANCE SHEET 51B N.W. EDITION 7.A. 1/20.000 Instruction to Battalions of 12th Infantry Brigade. Drill and company training. 3 other ranks reinforcements from Base.	
	9th.		Carrying on work as above. 2/Lieut. R.E. MILES and 2/Lieut. A.H. GADD joined company from BASE.	
	10th.		N.C.O's and Sappers attached to 12th Infantry Brigade Battalions rejoin company. Rest day. Inspections of arms equipment, drill with Box Respirators. Major J.B. HALL Struck off strength.	
ARRAS.	11th.		Company moved from TILLOY-LES-HERMAVILLE, dismounted sections and Headquarters to G.16.a.4.4. mounted section to G.16.a.4.4.	
BLANGY.	12th.		Dismounted sections and Headquarters moved from ARRAS to BLANGY.	
	13th.		Officers and N.C.O's reconnoitering line. No. 1 Section on night work, mined dugouts at I.19.c.1.5. clearing and opening out entrances.	
	14th.		Sections on work as follows :- Dugouts at I.19.c.1.5., and I.19.c.1.4½. Wiring Intermediate Line. Improving accomodation in camp and cleaning up.	
	15th.		Dugouts at I.19.c.1.5.; I.19.c.0.5½.; wiring intermediate line, erecting cupola shelters at H.23.c.2.7., Improving Brigade Headquarters accomodation at H.23.b.4.9., making notice for Area Commandant.	
	16th.		Carrying on work as above.	

[signature] Capt.
for O/C 526th (Durham) Field Co. R.E.

Army Form C. 2118.

WAR DIARY
or
INTELLIGENCE SUMMARY.

526th (Durham) Field Co. R.E.

(Erase heading not required.)

Instructions regarding War Diaries and Intelligence Summaries are contained in F. S. Regs., Part II. and the Staff Manual respectively. Title pages will be prepared in manuscript.

Place	Date	Hour	Summary of Events and Information	Remarks and references to Appendices
BLANGY.	1917.			
	JUNE 17th.		Sections on work as follows :- dugouts at I.19.c.1.5., I.19.c.0.5½., dressing station at H.30.d.2.5., elephant shelter at H.30.d.1.4., wiring intermediate line, cupola shelters at H.23.c.2.7., work on Brigade Headquarters at H.23.b.4.9., notice boards for Area Commandant.	
	18th.		Carrying on work as above.	

J M Dud Capt.
for O/C 526th (Durham) Field Co. R.E.

A5834 Wt.W4973/M687 750,000 8.16 D.D.&L.Ltd. Forms/C2118/13.

Army Form C. 2118.

WAR DIARY
or
INTELLIGENCE SUMMARY

526th (Durham) Field Co. R.E.

(Erase heading not required.)

Instructions regarding War Diaries and Intelligence Summaries are contained in F. S. Regs., Part II. and the Staff Manual respectively. Title pages will be prepared in manuscript.

Place	Date	Hour	Summary of Events and Information	Remarks and references to Appendices
BLANGY.	1917. JUNE 19th.		MAP REFERENCE. Major V.E. PURCELL from 15th Corps Headquarters, took over Command of Company. Sections on work as follows :- Construction of dugouts in CRUMP TRENCH at I.19.c.1.5., I.19.c.0.5½., AID POST at H.30.d.4.9., wiring intermediate line, erecting camouflage at railway H.23.b.3.2., work on cupola shelters at H.23.c.2.7., erecting elephant shelter in CORONA TRENCH, work on Brigade Headquarters at H.23.b.4.9. completed, dugout in ELBOW TRENCH I.25.d.½.8. for Machine Gun Company, repairing REIVES ROAD.	
	20th.		Dugouts in CRUMP TRENCH at I.19.c.1.5., I.19.c.0.5½., AID POST at H.30.d.4.9., elephant shelter at H.30.d.2½.5½., cupola shelters at H.23.c.2.7., dugout in ELBOW TRENCH I.25.d.½.8. erecting elephant shelter in CORONA TRENCH.	
	21st.		Carrying on work as above, wiring intermediate line, erecting camouflage at H.23.b.3.2. completed. Lieut. H.T. FOSTER, 2/Lieut. M. SWALES joined company from Base.	
	22nd.		Sections on works as follows :- Construction of dugouts in CRUMP TRENCH at I.19.c.1.5., I.19.c.0.5½ completed. AID POST at H.30.d.4.9., elephant shelter at H.30.d.2½.5½., wiring intermediate line, cupola shelters at H.23.c.2.7., company Headquarters at I.13.d.7.1. dugout in ELBOW TRENCH at I.25.d.½.8. for Machine Gun Company, repairing REIVES ROAD.	
	23rd		Carrying on work as above.	
	24th		Carrying on work as above.	

V.E. Purcell
Major.
O/C 526th (Durham) Field Co. R.E.

Army Form C.2118.

WAR DIARY
or
INTELLIGENCE SUMMARY.   526th (Durham) Field Co. R.E.
(Erase heading not required.)

Instructions regarding War Diaries and Intelligence Summaries are contained in F. S. Regs., Part II. and the Staff Manual respectively. Title pages will be prepared in manuscript.

Place	Date	Hour	Summary of Events and Information	Remarks and references to Appendices
BLANGY.	1917. JUNE 25th.		Sections on work as follows :- dugouts in CRUMP TRENCH at I.19.c.0.5½., elephant shelter at H.24.b.8.0., wiring intermediate line, making screens and camouflage, shelters at H.23.c.2.7., shelters at I.13.d.7.1., dugout in ELBOW TRENCH I.25.d.2.8., wiring WELFORD TRENCH, and CORDITE TRENCH. Capt. T.H. WEIR attached to 406th (Renfrew) Field Co. R.E.	
	26th.		Carrying on work as above. Supervising digging of CUSP TRENCH from H.36.b.9.3. to H.36.c.8.5.	
	27th.		Carrying on work as above.	
	28th.		Carrying on work as above.	
	29th.		Carrying on work as above.	
	30th.		Carrying on work as above.	

B.E. Purcell
Major,
O/C 526th (Durham) Field Co. R.E.

WAR DIARY

By

The Officer Commanding 526th (Durham) Field Co. R.E.

For

JULY 1917.

Army Form C. 2118

WAR DIARY
or
~~INTELLIGENCE SUMMARY~~

526th (Durham) Field Co. R.E.

(Erase heading not required.)

Instructions regarding War Diaries and Intelligence Summaries are contained in F.S. Regs., Part II. and the Staff Manual respectively. Title pages will be prepared in manuscript.

Place	Date	Hour	Summary of Events and Information	Remarks and references to Appendices
	JULY 1917.		MAP REFERENCE : PLOUVAIN, parts of 51B. N.W. & S.W. 1/10,000.	
BLANGY. (H.19.c.5.8)	1st.		Strength of Coy:- Nine Officers 210 other ranks. Sections on work in forward area as follows :- Constructing shelters in COLOMBO TRENCH, at I.14.c.4.0., erecting elephant shelter for Brigade Headquarters at H.23.c.2.7., shelter for Company Headquarters at I.23.d.7.1., erecting cookhouses and latrines for Brigade Headquarters., digging CUSP TRENCH from I.19.c.2.4. to I.19.a.7.3. Captain T.F. WEIR attached to 406th (Renfrew) Field Co. R.E.	
	2nd.		Constructing shelters in COLOMBO TRENCH, I.14. c.4.0., making and erecting frames for gas curtains for Battalion Headquarters at H.24.b.9.4., erecting 6 small elephant shelters H.23.c.4.7., erecting shelter for Company Headquarters in CORONA TRENCH at I.23.d.7.1., mined dugout in CABBAGE TRENCH for Company Headquarters at I.14.c.1.2., mined dugout for Machine Gunners in CEYLON TRENCH at I.19.b.6.7., digging CUSP TRENCH with Infantry party from I.19.c.2.4. to I.19.a.7.3.	
	3rd.		Carrying on work as above. 6 small elephant shelters at H.23.c.4.7. completed.	
	4th.		Constructing shelters in COLOMBO TRENCH, I.14.c.4.0., Fixing of gas curtains for Battalion Headquarters at H.24.b.9.4. completed. Erecting 6 small elephant shelters at H.23.c.4.7., Mined dugout for Company Headquarters in CABBAGE TRENCH at I.14.c.1.2., mined shelter for Machine Gunners in COLOMBO TRENCH at I.20.a.4.5., mined dugout for Machine Gunners in CEYLON TRENCH at I.19.b.6.7., digging CUSP TRENCH. XX Wiring CORONA TRENCH.	
	5th.		Carrying on work as above. 2/Lieut. A.J. BEST joined company from ENGLAND. Attached to 406th (Renfrew) Field Co. 1 other rank reinforcement from No. 5 Reinforcement Co. R.E.	

V.S. Purcell — Major,
O/C 526th (Durham) Field Co. R.E.

Army Form C. 2118.

WAR DIARY
or
~~INTELLIGENCE~~ SUMMARY

(Erase heading not required.)

526th (Durham) Field Co. R.E.

Instructions regarding War Diaries and Intelligence
Summaries are contained in F.S. Regs., Part II.
and the Staff Manual respectively. Title pages
will be prepared in manuscript.

Place	Date	Hour	Summary of Events and Information	Remarks and references to Appendices
BLANGY. I.19.c.5.8)	1917. JULY			
	6th.		Sections on work as follows :- Constructing mined shelters in COLOMBO TRENCH at I.14.c.4.0. and I.20.a.3.7., laying trench boards in CABBAGE TRENCH, wiring CORONA TRENCH, mined dugout for Company Headquarters in CABBAGE TRENCH at I.14.c.1.2., mined shelter for Machine Gunners in COLOMBO TRENCH at I.20.a.4.5., mined dugout in CEYLON TRENCH at I.19.b.6.7., Mined dugout in CORONA TRENCH at I.19.b.5.7., digging CUSP TRENCH with Infantry Party from I.19.c.2.4. to I.19.a.7.3.; erecting elephant shelter at H.23.c.4.8.	
	7th.		Carrying on work as above. 5 other ranks reinforcements from No. 5 Reinforcement Co. R.E.	
	8th.		Mined shelters in COLOMBO TRENCH completed. Laying trench boards in CABBAGE TRENCH, wiring CORONA TRENCH, mined dugouts in Railway Embankment at H.23.c.4.7. and H.23.c.4.8., elephant shelter at H.23.c.4.8., mined dugout for Company Headquarters in CABBAGE TRENCH at I.14.c.1.2., mined shelter in COLOMBO at I.20.a.4.5., mined dugout in CEYLON TRENCH at I.19.b.5.7., mined dugout CORONA at I.19.b.5.7., Captain T.H. WEIR rejoined company from 406th (Renfrew) Field Co. R.E.	
	9th.		Carrying on work as above. 2/Lieut. A.J. BEST rejoined company from 406th (Renfrew) Field Co. R.E.	
	10th.		Laying trench boards in CABBAGE TRENCH, mined dugout in Railway Embankment at H.23.c.4.7., mined dugouts at H.23.c.4.8., mined dugout for Company Headquarters in CABBAGE TRENCH at I.14.c.1.2., mined shelter in COLOMBO TRENCH at I.20.a.4.5. digging CUSP TRENCH	

R.L. Purcell
Major,
O/C 526th (Durham) Field Co. R.E.

Army Form C. 2118.

WAR DIARY
or
INTELLIGENCE SUMMARY 526th (Durham) Field Co. R.E.

(Erase heading not required.)

Instructions regarding War Diaries and Intelligence Summaries are contained in F. S. Regs. Part II and the Staff Manual respectively. Title pages will be prepared in manuscript.

Place	Date	Hour	Summary of Events and Information	Remarks and references to Appendices
BLANGY. (H.19.c.5.8)	1917. July			
	11th.		Constructing 3 shelters lined with mining frames in COLOMBO TRENCH at I.20.a.4.9., I.20.a.4.8., I.20.a.5.5., wiring CORONA TRENCH, mined dugout H.23.c.4.7., mined dugout H.23.c.4.8., mined dugout for Company Headquarters in CABBAGE TRENCH at I.14.c.1.2., mined shelter for Machine Gunners in COLOMBO at I.20.a.4.5., mined dugout CEYLON at I.14.b.6.7. mined dugout CORONA I.19.b.5.7., digging CUSP TRENCH.	
	12th.		Laying Trench boards in CABBAGE TRENCH, mined dugouts H.23.c.4.7. & H.23.c.4.8., mined dugout for Company Headquarters in CABBAGE TRENCH at I.14.c.1.2., mined dugout in CEYLON I.19.b.6.7., mined dugout CORONA I.19.b.5.7., large elephant shelter H.23.c.4.7. 2/Lieut. A.J. BEST attached to 406th (Renfrew) Field Co. for duty.	
	13th.		Constructing three shelters lined with mining frames in COLOMBO TRENCH at I.20.a.4.9., I.20.a.4.8., I.20.a.5.5., erecting large English shelter in CRUMP TRENCH at I.19.c.13.4. Shelter in CORONA at I.13.d.0.7. completed. Wiring CORONA TRENCH. Mined dugouts in Railway Embankment at I.23.c.4.7. and H.23.c.4.8. Battalion Headquarters dugout at H.23.c.7.6., mined dugout for Company Headquarters in CABBAGE TRENCH at I.14.c.1.2., mined dugouts in CEYLON TRENCH at I.19.b.6.7, CORONA TRENCH I.19.b.5.7.	
	14th.		Carrying on work as above.	
	15th.		Carrying on work as above.	
	16th.		Carrying on work as above. 3 other ranks reinforcements from No. 4 Reinforcement Co. R.E.	
	17th.		Carrying on work as above.	

[signature]
Major,
O/C 526th (Durham) Field Co. R.E.

Army Form C.2118.

WAR DIARY
or
INTELLIGENCE SUMMARY. 526th (Durham) Field Co. R.E.

(Erase heading not required.)

Instructions regarding War Diaries and Intelligence Summaries are contained in F. S. Regs., Part II. and the Staff Manual respectively. Title pages will be prepared in manuscript.

Place	Date	Hour	Summary of Events and Information	Remarks and references to Appendices
BLANGY. (H.19.c.5.8.)	1917. July 18th.		Sections on work as follows :- Construction of 3 shelters lined with moning frames in COLOMBO at I.20.a.4.5., I.20.a.4.9., I.20.a.5.5. completed. Erecting English shelter in CRUMP TRENCH at I.19.c.1.4., wiring CORONA TRENCH, mined dugouts in Railway Embankment at H.23.c.4.7., H.23.c.7.8., H.23.c.4.8., mined dugout for Company Headquarters in CABBAGE TRENCH at I.14.c.1.12., mined shelter in COLOMBO at I.20.a.4.5., mined dugout in CEYLON at I.19.b.6.7., mined dugout in CORONA at I.19.b.5.7.,	
	19th.		Carrying on work as above, constructing 4 shelters in CORONA at I.19.b.5.7., I.19.b.6.9., I.13.d.7.0., I.13.d.7½.2½.,	
	20th.		Carrying on work as above. Casualties, 2 other ranks killed by Shell fire.	
	21st.		Carrying on work as above. XXXXXXXXXXXXXXXXXXXXXX.Elephant shelter in Crump trench I.19.c.1.4. completed.	
	22nd.		Fixing boxes for holding 4 boxes of grenades in front system, and carrying on work as above.	
	23rd.		Carrying on work as above.	

R Purcell
Major,
O/C 526th (Durham) Field Co. R.E.

WAR DIARY
or
~~INTELLIGENCE~~ **SUMMARY.**

(Erase heading not required.)

Army Form C. 2118.

526th (Durham) Field Co. R.E.

Place	Date	Hour	Summary of Events and Information	Remarks and references to Appendices
BLANGY. (H.19.c. 5.8)	1917. July 24th.		Constructing shelters limed with mining frames in CORONA TRENCH at I.19.b.5.9., I.19.b.6.9., I.13.d.7.2., I.13.d.7.0., fixing boxes for holding 4 boxes of grenades in front system, erecting O.P. off CUSP TRENCH at I.19.c.5².7²., wiring CORONA TRENCH, constructing mined dugouts at H.23.c.4.7., H.23.c.4.8., H.23.c.7.8., I.14.c.1.2., I.19.b.6.7., I.19.b.5.7., Mined shelter in COLOMBO at I.20.a.4.5., erecting O.P. in gantry ROEUX WOOD at I.19.c.7.3.	
	25th.		Carrying on work as above. Wiring CORONA TRENCH. Casualties, 1 other rank wounded.	
	26th.		Shelters in CORONA TRENCH completed. O.P. of CUSP TRENCH completed. Carrying on remainder of work. Wiring COLOMBO TRENCH.	
	27th.		O.P. in ROEUX completed. Carrying on with remainder of work. Casualties, 2 other ranks killed and 2 wounded by shell fire.	
	28th.		Fixing gas curtains in CRETE TRENCH for Battalion Headquarters, fixing boxes for S.A.A. in COLOMBO, CABBAGE & CORONA TRENCHES, mined dugouts at H.23.c.4.7., H.23.c.4.8., H23.c.7.8., I.14.c.1.2., I.19.b.6.7., mined shelter I.20.a.4.5., camouflaging at H.23.c.4.7. [Mu-book did Abouts]	
	29th.		Carrying on work as above. Lined dugout for Company Headquarters in CABBAGE TRENCH at I.14.c.1.2. completed.	
	30th.		Carrying on work as above. Fixing of gas curtains to Battalion Headquarters completed.	
	31st.		Carrying on work as above. Strength in [France] 10 officers 202 oth ranks	

B Purcell
Major.
O/C 526th (Durham) Field Co. R.E.

WAR   DIARY

BY THE OFFICER COMMANDING 526th (DURHAM) FIELD CO. R.E.

FOR MONTH OF AUGUST 1917.

Army Form C. 2118.

WAR DIARY
or
INTELLIGENCE SUMMARY. 526th (Durham) Field Co. R.E.

(Erase heading not required.)

Instructions regarding War Diaries and Intelligence
Summaries are contained in F. S. Regs., Part II.
and the Staff Manual respectively. Title pages
will be prepared in manuscript.

Place	Date	Hour	Summary of Events and Information	Remarks and references to Appendices
BLANG. H.19.c. 5.8.	1917. AUGUST.		MAP REFERENCE :- TRENCH MAP FRANCE, SHEET 51B N.W. Edition 7 A. Scale 1/20,000.	
	1st.		Strength of Company Officers 8, other ranks 202. Sections on work as follows :- Fixing S.A.A. boxes in CABBAGE, COLOMA and CROFT TRENCHES. Wiring COLOMBO TRENCH, mined dugouts at I.23.c.4.7., H.23.c.4.8., I.19.b.7.6., I.19.b.5.7., Fixing of S.A.A. boxes completed. Wiring COLOMBO, work on mined dugouts.	
	2nd.			
	3rd.		Carrying on work mined dugouts, erecting large English shelter in CRUMP TRENCH for wireless Operators, making shelters lined with frames in CORONA TRENCH.	
	4th.		Carrying on work as above.	
	5th.		Carrying on work as same above.	
	6th.		Carrying on work as above.	
	7th.		Carrying on work as above.	
	8th.		Carrying on work as above.	

[signature] Major,
O/C 526th (Durham) Field Co. R.E.

Army Form C. 2118.

WAR DIARY
or
INTELLIGENCE SUMMARY. 526th (Durham) Field Co. R.E.

(Erase heading not required.)

Instructions regarding War Diaries and Intelligence Summaries are contained in F.S. Regs., Part II. and the Staff Manual respectively. Title pages will be prepared in manuscript.

Place	Date	Hour	Summary of Events and Information	Remarks and references to Appendices
PLANG. H.19.c.5.8.	1917. August. 9th.		Sections on work :- mined dugouts H.23.c.7.8., H.23.c.4.8., I.19.b.7.6., I.19.b.5.7., erecting large English shelter in CRUMP TRENCH H.24.d.3.8. for wireless operator, making shelters lined with frames in COLOMBO trench. Mined dugout at H.23.c.4.7 completed. Wiring COLOMBO TRENCH, camouflaging Railway Cutting H.23.c.4.7.	
	10th.		Carrying on work as above.	
	11th.		Carrying on work as above.	
	12th.		Carrying on work as above. Casualties. 1 other Rank killed in action, by shell fire.	
	13th.		Carrying on work as stated for 12th. 1 Reinforcement joined company from No. 4 Reinforcement Co. R.E.	
	14th.		Mined dugouts H.22.c.7.3., I.19.b.7.6., I.19.b.5.7., Mined dugout at H.23.c.4.3. completed erecting elephant shelter at H.24d.3.8. making shelters lined with frames in COLOMBO.	
	15th.		Carrying on work as above.	

O/C 526th (Durham) Field Co. R.E.

Army Form C. 2118.

WAR DIARY
or
INTELLIGENCE SUMMARY
526th (Durham) Field Co. R.E.

(Erase heading not required.)

Instructions regarding War Diaries and Intelligence Summaries are contained in F. S. Regs., Part II. and the Staff Manual respectively. Title pages will be prepared in manuscript.

Place	Date	Hour	Summary of Events and Information	Remarks and references to Appendices
BIACHE, H.19.c.5.8.	1917. AUGUST. 16th.		Sections on work as follows :- Mined dugouts at I.19.b.5.7., I.19.b.5.7., erecting bunks in dugout at H.23.c.4.8., erecting English shelter for Wireless Operator at H.24.d.8.8. making shelters lined with frames in COLOMBO and CROFT TRENCHES, wiring COLOMBO TRENCH, widening, deepening and cleaning berm CEYLON TRENCH.	
	17th.		Carrying on work as above. Erecting Pump in well at ROEUX.I.19.b.3.5.	
	18th.		Carrying on work as above.	
	19th.		Erecting bunks in dugout at H.23.c.4.8. completed. Mined dugouts at I.19.b.7.6., I.19.b.5.7., making shelters lined with frames at "D" Post, wiring COLOMBO TRENCH, erecting English shelter at H.24.d.8.8. Fixing and erecting Pump in well at ROEUX I.19.b.3.5. Nos. 1 & 2 Sections moved from H.19.c.5.8. to H.19.c.5.8.	
	20th.		Pump for well in ROEUX completed. Erecting and fixing "A" frames in SCABRAID TRENCH, making shelters lined with frames at "C" and "D" posts, wiring COLOMBO TRENCH, deepening, widening, and cleaning berm CABBAGE and CEYLON TRENCHES, mined dugouts at I.19.b.765., I.19.b.5.7.; 1 other rank reinforcement from 230th Army Troop Co. R.E. 1 other ranks died of wounds received in action 27-7-17.	
	21st.		Carrying on work as above.	

[signature] Capt. R.E.
for O/C 526th (Durham) Field Co. R.E.

Army Form C. 2118.

WAR DIARY
or
INTELLIGENCE SUMMARY.   526th (Durham) Field Co. R.E.

(Erase heading not required.)

Instructions regarding War Diaries and Intelligence Summaries are contained in F. S. Regs., Part II. and the Staff Manual respectively. Title pages will be prepared in manuscript.

Place	Date	Hour	Summary of Events and Information	Remarks and references to Appendices
	1917.			
BLANGY.	22nd.		Fitting "A" frames, revetting and trench boarding SCABBARD TRENCH, making frames and fitting gas curtains to dugouts in LONE COPSE, WELLFORD TRENCH, making shelters lined with frames at "C" and "D" posts, wiring COLOMBO TRENCH, deepening and grading CABBAGE and CEYLON TRENCH, erecting shelter in trench leading to and at sump in ROACH, mined dugouts at I.19.b.5.7.	
F.19.c.5.8.	23rd.		Carrying on work as above.	
	24th.		Fixing "A" frames, revetting and laying trench boards in SCABBARD TRENCH, making shelters lined with frames in ELBOW TRENCH and "C" post, fixing gas curtains to dugouts at H.23.c.4.7. and H.23.c.4.8., and LONE COPSE, wiring COLOMB TRENCH, deepening, widening and cleaning berm CABBAGE and CEYLON TRENCHES, excavating for 2 English shelters for Aid post in CRUMP. Mined dugouts at I.19.b.7.6., I.19.b.5.7.	
	25th.		Carrying on work as above.	
	26th.		Carrying on work as above.	

[signature] Capt. R.E.
for O/C 526th (Durham) Field Co. R.E.

Army Form C. 2118.

WAR DIARY
or
INTELLIGENCE SUMMARY. 526th (Durham) Field Co. R.E.

(Erase heading not required.)

Instructions regarding War Diaries and Intelligence Summaries are contained in F.S. Regs., Part II. and the Staff Manual respectively. Title pages will be prepared in manuscript.

Place	Date	Hour	Summary of Events and Information	Remarks and references to Appendices
BLANGY. I.19.c.5.3.	1917. August. 27th.		Fixing "A" frames, and laying trench boards in SCABBARD TRENCH, fixing frames and gas curtains to dugouts occupied, lining shelters with frames in FINGER and WELLFORD TRENCHES and "B" post. Erecting 2 English shelters for Aid post in CRUMP, supervising construction of Trench Mortar Emplacement in CUSP TRENCH, deepening widening and cleaning berm CABBAGE and CEYLON TRENCHES, fixing bunks in elephant shelter in CEYLON TRENCH, at I.19.b.45.80., mined dugout at I.19.b.7.6. completed. mined dugout I.19.b.5.7.	
	28th.		Carrying on work as above. No 3 Section resting and training.	
	29th.		Carrying on work as above.	
			Making shelters lined with frames in ELBOW TRENCH and "B" post, bunking dugout in SCABBARD TRENCH, and fixing gas frames and curtains, erecting S.A.A. boxes in front line system, erecting 2 English shelters in CRUMP TRENCH for Aid post, wiring COLOMBO TRENCH, deepening widening and cleaning berm, fixing "A" frames in CABBAGE and CEYLON TRENCHES, fixing gas curtains to dugouts in CEYLON TRENCH, bunking elephant shelter in CEYLON TRENCH completed, supervising construction of Trench Mortar Emplacement in CUSP TRENCH, mined dugout at I.19.b.5.7. completed.	
	30th.		Carrying on work as above. Nos 3 and 4 Sections resting and training.	
	31st.		Carrying on work as above.	

for O/C 526th (Durham) Field Co. R.E.

Capt. R.E.

WAR DIARY

of

The Officer Commanding, 526th (Durham) Field Co. R.E.

From 1st September to 30th September 1917.

Army Form C. 2118.

WAR DIARY
or
INTELLIGENCE SUMMARY

(Erase heading not required.)

526th (Durham) Field Co. R.E.

Instructions regarding War Diaries and Intelligence Summaries are contained in F. S. Regs., Part II. and the Staff Manual respectively. Title pages will be prepared in manuscript.

Place	Date	Hour	Summary of Events and Information	Remarks and references to Appendices
BLANGY. F.19.c. 5.3.	September. 1st.		REFERENCE MAP. TRENCH MAP - FRANCE, SHEET 51B N.W. Edition 7 A. 1/20.000. STRENGTH OF COMPANY 8 Officers 208 other ranks. Nos 1 and 2 Sections working in Forward Area. Bunking dugouts in SCABBARD TRENCH, fitting S.A. loops in front system, fitting A frames and trench boarding SCABBARD TRENCH, making shelters lined with frames in front system, erecting elephant shelter for Aid post in CRUMP, wiring COLOMBO TRENCH, deepening widening and clearing berm in CABBAGE and CEYLON TRENCHES, fixing frames and gas curtains to dugouts, supervising erection of TRENCH MORTAR EMPLACEMENT in CUSP TRENCH. Nos 3 and 4 Sections erecting horse standings and making road at Railway Triangle.	
	2nd.		Carrying on work as above.	
	3rd.		Carrying on work as above.	
	4th.		Carrying on work as above. Work handed over to 74th Field Co. R.E. No. 3 Section proceeded to RANSART for erection of R.E. Camp.	
RANSART.	5th.		Company moved from BLANGY (H.19.c.588.) to RANSART, relieved by 74th Field Co. R.E.	
	6th.		Company employed on erection of R.E. Camp.	
	7th.		Company employed on erection of R.E. Camp.	
	8th.		Company employed on erection of R.E. Camp.	
	9th.		Rest day, Inspections of arms, equipments, P.H. Helmets and Box respirators and Church parade.	

O/C 526th (Durham) Field Co. R.E.

Army Form C. 2118.

WAR DIARY
or
INTELLIGENCE SUMMARY. 526th (Durham) Field Co. R.E.

(Erase heading not required.)

Instructions regarding War Diaries and Intelligence Summaries are contained in F.S. Regs., Part II. and the Staff Manual respectively. Title pages will be prepared in manuscript.

Place	Date	Hour	Summary of Events and Information	Remarks and references to Appendices
	September.			
RANSART.	10th.		Company Training as follows :- Route marching, Section drill and rifle exercises, pontooning, demolitions, wiring, trestle bridging and general field works. Lectures given by C.R.E. 4th Division to Officers and N.C.O's.	
	11th.		Training as above.	
	12th.		Training as above.	
	13th.		Musketry on Range.	
	14th.		Training as sitted for 10th.	
	15th.		Training as sitted for 10th.	
	16th.		Inspection of arms, equipment etc. and Church parades.	
	17th.		Company resting owing to Inoculation.	
	18th.		Company moved from RANSART to PAS.	
	19th.		Company parade for hot baths, and preparing for move.	
	20th 21st.		Mounted Section parade at 8-0 a.m. dismounted Section at 10-0 a.m. and proceeded to MONDICOURT, entrained at MONDICOURT at 12 noon, and arrived at HOPOUTRE, detrained and marched to FUTIOWES CAMP (F.10.a.5.2.) near PROVEN at 1-45 a.m.	

Army Form C. 2118.

WAR DIARY
or
INTELLIGENCE SUMMARY

526th (Durham) Field Co. R.E.

(Erase heading not required.)

Place	Date	Hour	Summary of Events and Information	Remarks and references to Appendices
PUTLOWS CAMP. F.10.a.5.2.	22/9/17.		Inspection of Arms, Equipment, etc., and Section Drill.	
	23rd.		Church Parades.	
"	24th.		Sections Nos. 1 & 2 carried out training with Weldon Trestles. Sections Nos. 3 & 4 on Pontooning. Afternoon. Lectures by Section Officers on Map and Compass Reading.	
"	25th.		Sections Nos. 1 & 2 Pontoon training. Sections Nos 3 & 4 with Weldon Trestles. Afternoon, Company Drill.	
"	26th		Company wagons washed and overhauled. Pontoons leafed on wagons. Major V.B.PURCHI. R.E. proceeded to Base. Captain T.F.WEIR.R.E. assumed command of Company.	
"	27th		Section Drill and Rifle Exercises under Section Officers. Also Inspection of Gas Appliances. 2nd Lieut GADD proceeded to forward area and took over work from 96th(Field) Co.R.E.	
"	28th		Dismounted Section parade in full marching order at 7-30 a.m. ready to move off. Dismounted Section marched to PROVEN Siding, entrained and proceeded to ELVERINGHE, detrained and marched to Delta Camp situated at B.23.b.6.4. (Ref. Sheet 28 N.W.) Mounted Section paraded at 8-30 a.m. and proceeded by march route to Glette Camp as mentioned above. Sections Nos 1 & 2 billeted at Nissen Hut Camp at B.20.d.8.8. relieved from 9th Field Co.R.E.	
B.23...6.4.	29th		Moved in at 3-0 p.m. 2nd Lieut. MORRIS R.E. joined Company. Relieved from 9th Field Co.R.E.	
			Sections Nos 1 & 2 moved from Nissen Hut Camp at B.20.d.8.8. to Shelter Camp at B.25.b.6.4. Sections Nos 3 & 4 and working party of attached Infantry working in forward area at mill carrying trench boards from BROAD STREET R.E.Dump (C.8.a.8.6.) to Rat House and of train bearding at C.29.b.9.2. Party heavily shelled. 2 Sappers slightly wounded, remained at duty.	
"	30th.		Sections Nos. 1 & 2 on day working parties. No.1 Section laying trench boards from U.5.a.1.5. to U.5.c.5.5. (about 110 yards). Repairing trench boards in Sunken Road about U.5.b.central	

Army Form C. 2118.

WAR DIARY
or
INTELLIGENCE SUMMARY

526th (Durham) Fld. Co. R.E.

(Erase heading not required.)

Instructions regarding War Diaries and Intelligence Summaries are contained in F. S. Regs., Part II. and the Staff Manual respectively. Title pages will be prepared in manuscript.

Place	Date	Hour	Summary of Events and Information	Remarks and references to Appendices
B.23.b.6.4.	30th contd.		Section No.2. 5 excavations completed for Small Elephant Shelters at JOLIE FARM (C.9.a.4.8.) 4 excavations 75% completed. Carrying 5 Shelters from YARD Dump to site. Sections Nos.3 & 4 on light work. Traced trench board track from FAT MOUSE to a position near WHITE MILL. (U.24.a.5.2.) Approximately 558 yards of trenchboard track laid.	
			Strength of Company on 30th instant :- 8 Officers, 207 other ranks.	

J.W.W.
Captain, R.E.
O.C., 526th (Durham) Field Co. R.E.

WAR DIARY

of

The Officer Commanding, 526th (Durham) Field Co.R.E.

From 1st October to 31st October,1917.

Army Form C. 2118.

WAR DIARY
or
INTELLIGENCE SUMMARY.
(Erase heading not required.)

Instructions regarding War Diaries and Intelligence Summaries are contained in F. S. Regs., Part II and the Staff Manual respectively. Title pages will be prepared in manuscript.

Place	Date	Hour	Summary of Events and Information	Remarks and references to Appendices
Ref.Sheet BELGIUM 28.N.W. B.23.b.6.4.	1/10/17.		Strength of Company of 1st October,1917.:- 8 Officers, 207 other ranks. Day parties. Laying trenchboard track from the INGS(C.4.a.6.8.) to C.4.b.4.6. - 300 yards completed. Laying trenchboard track over stream from the INGS to CEMENT HOUSE Aid Post. 5 Excavations completed at JOLLIE FARM (C.9.a.4.8.) - total completed 8. Carrying shelters from HARD DUMP. to site. Night parties. Covered stores from HARD DUMP to MILITARY RIDGE by Company Transport, materials been carried forward to WHITE TRENCH (Now Dump). 100 yards of trenchboards pulled up at RAT HOUSE during day and laid on the earth track of the 4th Division. Casualties for 1st inst:- 1 o.r. wounded.	
"	2nd.		Day parties. Laying double track trenchboards in SUNKEN ROAD between C.8.a.8.2. and C.8.b.6.5. - 275 yards completed. Laying trenchboard track from C.4.b.2.8. to C.4.b.8.9. - 300 yards completed. Night parties. Taped out new trenchboard track:- U.29.c.5.6. - BIRD HOUSE - U.29.d.8.6. - Battalion Headquarters U.29.b.7.9. Laid trenchboards to BIRD HOUSE. Casualties for 2nd inst:- 2 o.rs. killed. 4 o.rs. wounded.	
"	3rd.		Day parties. Took up trenchboard track from C.4.b.3.6. to MILITARY BRIDGE (STEENBEEK) and completed relaying of same from C.4.b.5.1 to MILITARYBRIDGE (STEENBEEK). 3 Shelters completed at JOLLIE FARM, making total of 9 Shelters completed. 2 excavations completed ready for shelters. Night parties. Carrying and laying trenchboards between U.29.c.3.8. and U.29.a.9.5. 250 yards of track laid. Casualties for 3rd inst:- 1 o.r. killed.	
"	4th.		4th Division (forming part of XIVth Corps) attacked at 6.20 a.m.	

A5834 Wt.W4973/M687 750,000 8/16 D. D. & L. Ltd. Forms/C.2118/13

Army Form C. 2118.

WAR DIARY
or
~~INTELLIGENCE SUMMARY~~
(Erase heading not required.)

Instructions regarding War Diaries and Intelligence Summaries are contained in F.S. Regs., Part II. and the Staff Manual respectively. Title pages will be prepared in manuscript.

Place	Date	Hour	Summary of Events and Information	Remarks and references to Appendices
B.23.b.6.4.	4th contd.		Track traced off with tapes to 200 yards beyond KANGAROO TRENCH. Notice boards erected at 60 yards intervals and at crossings of trenches. 150 yards of trenchboards laid. Direction of track is BIRD HOUSE - U.29.d.5.4. to U.24.b.5.0. Maintaining track from U.29.c.5.6. to BIRD HOUSE. 25 trenchboards transported to Cross Roads past MILITARY BRIDGE. Casualties for 4th inst:- 2nd Lieut. A.J.BEST, wounded. 1 o.r. wounded.	
"	5th.		Day parties. Relaying trenchboards from C.4.b.4.4. to U.29.c.3.7. Night Parties. Carrying trenchboards from bottom of trenchboard track to BIRD HOUSE. 40 yards of track laid beyond WHITE HOUSE. Parties heavily shelled. Casualties for 5th inst:- 1 o.r. wounded.	
"	6th.		Track boards laid to a point 280 yards beyond KANGAROO Trench. 400 trenchboards and other material carried to Dump at WHITE TRENCH. Party maintaining track up to WHITE TRENCH. Casualties for 6th inst:- 1 o.r. wounded.	
"	7th.		Work in forward area handed over to 406th (Readjust) Field Company R.E. Took over work in rear area.	
"	8th.		Erecting Elephant Shelter at U.29.c.6.3. - completed. Making over Tramways. Maintainance party placed in CANDLE TRENCH. 5 trucks of material taken up. 180 yards of road prepared for lime. Track taped off to POELCAPPELLE Road. Improving line at BROAD STREET. Casualties for 8th inst:- Lieut. R.W.WILLIAMS, wounded.	
"	9th		4th Division (forming Part of XIVth Corps) attached at 5-20 a.m. Repairing and maintaining track (Tramway) 100 yards of Track laid, Head of track at U.29.b.3.9. (on road). 130 yards of road prepared for laying track, Head of track prepared	

Army Form C. 2118.

WAR DIARY
or
INTELLIGENCE SUMMARY.
(Erase heading not required.)

Place	Date	Hour	Summary of Events and Information	Remarks and references to Appendices
B.23.b.6.4.	9th contd.		Repairing and maintaining Track "B" (Trenchboard track)	
			Casualties for 9th inst:- NIL.	
"	10th		Repairing and maintaining Tramway Track. 210 yards of track prepared for laying rails. Road repaired up to U.23.d.3.3. Tramway materials transported by tramway from the ENGS to dump. Materials also transported by Company from BARD Dump. Repairing and maintaining Trenchboard Track "B" up to WHITE TRENCH.	
			Casualties for 10th inst:- NIL.	
"	11th.		Repairing and maintaining Tramway Track. Track laid up to a point at U.23.d.35.40. Tramway materials transported by Tramway and by Company Transport. Repairing and maintaining Trenchboard Track new up to WHITE TRENCH. Erecting camouflage screen at about C.3.c.central.	
			Casualties for 11th inst:- 2 o.rs. wounded.	
"	12th.		Handing over work to 207th Field Company R.E. Company moved to PORTLAND CAMP at X.28.a. Dismounted sections by train from ELVERDINGHE to PROVEN thence by march route. Transport proceeded by road.	
PORTLAND CAMP. X.28.a.	13th.		Company Resting.	
	14th.		Inspections, arms, equipment, and gas appliances. 2nd Lieut. W. HERBERT, joined Company.	
"	15th.		Company moved from PORTLAND CAMP at X.28.a to POPERINGHE.	
POPERINGHE.	16th.		Dismounted sections employed on cleaning of wagons, etc. Checking of stores, deficiencies reported. Baths parade.	

Army Form C. 2118.

WAR DIARY
or
INTELLIGENCE SUMMARY

(Erase heading not required.)

Instructions regarding War Diaries and Intelligence Summaries are contained in F.S. Regs., Part II. and the Staff Manual respectively. Title pages will be prepared in manuscript.

Place	Date	Hour	Summary of Events and Information	Remarks and references to Appendices
POPERINGHE.	17th½		Inspections, clean arms, equipment, gas appliances, etc.	
"	18th.		Company moved from POPERINGHE (BELGIUM) to WARQUETIN (FRANCE). Mounted Sections paraded at 1-30 a.m. and proceeded to entraining station (PESHROEK). Disbanded Sections paraded at 3-30 a.m. and proceeded to entraining station. Company detrained at MAROEUIL and marched to WARQUETIN.	
WARQUETIN.	19th.		Inspections, etc.	
"	20th.		Rifle exercises, Section Drill and Organised Recreation.	
"	21st.		Section Drill and Company Drill. Church Parades. Organised Recreation.	
"	22nd.		Company moved from WARQUETIN to Camp at N.2.d.5.7. (Ref.Sheet:- 51.b. 1/40,000). Mounted Section at C.23.d.3.9.	
N.2".d.5.7.	23rd.		Sections employed on the following work:- Building up Firebay with Sandbags in EAST RESERVE (C.1.d.F.3.) also repairing and laying trenchboards, repairing entrances to 2 Dug-outs. ORCHARD RESERVE (about C.1.d.6.7.) Revetting and repairing damage caused by shell fire. Advanced Dressing Station at corner of PICK AVE. and CUMBRIA Road, 6 bunks erected. SECRET TRENCH (C.1.c.5.9.) Excavating, deepening and widening new branch to Chateau. MONCHY CHATEAU. Excavating foundation for brick wall in cellar. Gun Boat Stores at A.1.c.25.4. Building up fronts of 2 Elephant Shelters. Cookhouses in ORCHARD RESERVE. Completed existing Cookhouse, excavation for 2nd. commenced. Cookhouse in FORK RESERVE. Excavation commenced. Maintainance of Duckboard track from Railhead Dump to entrance of CIRCLE Trench. Petrolled Water Pipe line from Lor FOSSY Ferr through GORDON AVENUE - PICK AVENUE - FORK RESERVE.	
".	24th.		Sections employed as follows:- Maintainance of EAST RESERVE and ORCHARD RESERVE.	

WAR DIARY or INTELLIGENCE SUMMARY

Army Form C. 2118.

Place	Date	Hour	Summary of Events and Information	Remarks and references to Appendices
M.2.d.5.7.	24th. (contd)		Advanced Dressing Station, 6 bunks erected, job completed. Gum Beet Shelters at A.1.c.2½.4. Fixing shelves. Maintenance of duckboard from Railhead Dump to entrance of CIRCLE TRENCH. SECRET TRENCH, Excavating, deepening and widening breach to Chateau. Patrolling Pipe Line.	
"	25th.		Sections employed as follows:- Revetting and general repairs in EAST and ORCHARD RESERVE. Making and fixing shelves in Gum Beet Stores at A.1.c.2½.4. Excavation for Cookhouses in ORCHARD RESERVE. Deepening and widening trench to Cookhouse in ORCHARD RESERVE. SECRET TRENCH deepening, widening and revetting. Patrolling Water Pipe Line. 2nd. LIEUT. A. J. BEST. Awarded THE DISTINGUISHED SERVICE ORDER. (Immediate award.) No.470717. Lee/Corpl. W. IRVING. Awarded The MILITARY MEDAL. (Immediate award.)	
"	26th.		Sections employed as follows:- Revetting and repairs in EAST and ORCHARD RESERVE. FORK RESERVE excavating for cookhouse, making born and clearing back excavation for cookhouse. Maintenance of CIRCLE TRENCH and duckboard track from Railhead Dump. Work on Gum Beet Shelters at A.1.c.2½.4. 75% completed. Excavation for cookhouse in ORCHARD RESERVE. SECRET TRENCH, deepening, widening and revetting, 15 yards deepened, 15 yards revetted. Girders fixed in cellars in trench. Patrolling Water Pipe Line. Theatre at SCHRAM BARRACKS, ARRAS, partitions demolished, harness racks taken down.	
"	27th.		Sections employed as follows:- EAST RESERVE, revetting, completed 1 traverse and 2 firebays. ORCHARD RESERVE, 34 yards revetted, 12 yards duckboards laid. Gum Beet Shelters at A.1.c.2½.4. 95% completed. CIRCLE TRENCH, maintenance, revetting frames fitted. Excavating for 4 cookhouses in FORK RESERVE. Excavating for cookhouse at A.D.S. in PICK AVENUE. SECRET TRENCH deepening, widening and revetting. Patrolling Water Pipe Line. Theatre at SCHRAM BARRACKS, stage frame erected and flooring commenced. Foundations laid for Solder recovery Kiln at ESTAMINET CORNER.	
"	28th.		Sections employed as follows:- Revetting and repairs in EAST and ORCHARD RESERVE. Gum Beet Shelters at A.1.3.2½.4. 95% completed. CIRCLE TRENCH, maintenance. Cookhouses FORK RESERVE. SECRET TRENCH, deepening, widening and revetting. Theatre at SCHRAM BARRACKS. Solder recovery Kiln at ESTAMINET CORNER. Patrolling Pipe Line. Repairs to BEAURAINS CAMP.	

Army Form C. 2118.

WAR DIARY
or
INTELLIGENCE SUMMARY.
(Erase heading not required.)

Instructions regarding War Diaries and Intelligence Summaries are contained in F. S. Regs., Part II. and the Staff Manual respectively. Title pages will be prepared in manuscript.

Place	Date	Hour	Summary of Events and Information	Remarks and references to Appendices
N.2.a.5.7.	29th.		Sections employed as follows:- Revetting and repairs in EAST and ORCHARD RESERVE, also in CANISTER and CIRCLE. Patrolling Water Pipe Line. Cookhouses in FORK RESERVE. Laying duckboards in front of Gum Boot Shelters. Cookhouses in PICK AVENUE. SECRET TRENCH, revetting, deepening and widening. Bunking at BEAURAINS CAMP. Theatre at SCHRAM BARRACKS. Solder recovery kiln at ESTAMINET CORNER.	
"	30th.		Sections employed as follows:- Revetting and repairs in EAST and ORCHARD RESERVE, also CIRCLE. Patrolling Water Pipe Line. Anchoring back revetting frames. Cookhouses in FORK RESERVE and PICK AVENUE. SECRET TRENCH, deepening, widening and revetting. General repairs at BEAURAINS CAMP. Theatre at SCHRAM BARRACKS. Kiln at ESTAMINET CORNER, 70% completed.	
"	31st.		Sections employed as follows:- Revetting and repairs in EAST RESERVE, ORCHARD RESERVE and CIRCLE TRENCH. Patrolling Water Pipe Line, and lagging water pipes. Anchoring back revetting frames. SECRET TRENCH, deepening, widening and revetting. Bunking, etc, at BEAURAINS CAMP. Kiln at ESTAMINET CORNER. Theatre at SCHRAM BARRACKS. Gum Boot Shelters at A.1.c.2½.8. Cookhouses in FORK RESERVE. Gum Boot Shelters in ORANGE AVENUE. Cookhouses in PICK AVENUE. Cookhouses of CIRCLE TRENCH. O.1.c.5.4½.	

Company Strength on 31st inst:- 7 Officers and 207 other ranks.

JWWest Major.R.E.
O.C., 526th (Durham) Field Company R.E.

WAR DIARY

of

The Officer Commanding, 526th (Durham) Field Co.R.E.

From 1st November to 30th November 1917.

Army Form C. 2118.

WAR DIARY
or
INTELLIGENCE SUMMARY.
(Erase heading not required.)

Instructions regarding War Diaries and Intelligence Summaries are contained in F. S. Regs., Part II. and the Staff Manual respectively. Title pages will be prepared in manuscript.

Place	Date	Hour	Summary of Events and Information	Remarks and references to Appendices
N.2.d.5.7. (Sheet 51.b.)	1/11/17.		Strength of Company:- 7 Officers and 207 other ranks.	
			Sections Nos 1, 2, and 3, employed as follows:- Maintainance and general repairs to ORCHARD RESERVE, EAST RESERVE, CIRCLE TRENCH; Patrolling Pipe Line; Deepening, widening and rivetting SECRET TRENCH; Gun Boot Shelters in ORANGE AVENUE; Cookhouses in FORK RESERVE and PICK AVENUE also CIRCLE TRENCH. Section No.4 employed at BEAURAINS CAMP, bunking and general repairs; Fitting up Theatre in ARRAS; Solder recovery kiln at ESTAMINET CORNER.	
"	2nd.		Same as for 1st November. Solder recovery kiln at ESTAMINET CORNER completed.	
"	3rd.		- do - " Cookhouse in PICK AVENUE completed.	
"	4th.		- do - do -	
"	5th.		- do - do -	
"	6th.		- do - do - Fixing Gas Curtain Frames in dug-outs. Theatre completed. One Section received instruction in use of LEWIS GUN. Two Sections - Inspections. Soup Kitchen commenced at N.6.a.3.1. Trench-board Track from SWORD LANE to ORANGE AVENUE - 340 yds down to be laid - 75% completed. One Section received instruction in use of LEWIS GUN. One Section - Instruction.	
"	7th.		- do - do - Trench-board Track completed. Commenced filling in Mined Craters on CAMBRIA ROAD. One Section received instruction in use of LEWIS GUN.	
"	8th.		- do - do -	
"	9th.		- do - do - No.1 Section resting.	

Army Form C. 2118.

WAR DIARY
or
INTELLIGENCE SUMMARY.
(Erase heading not required.)

Instructions regarding War Diaries and Intelligence Summaries are contained in F. S. Regs., Part II. and the Staff Manual respectively. Title pages will be prepared in manuscript.

Place	Date	Hour	Summary of Events and Information	Remarks and references to Appendices
N.2.d.5.7.	10th		Same as for 1st November.	
"	11th		- do - do -	
"	12th		- do - do -	Clearing cellar for OPP. in MONCHY.
"	13th		- do - do -	
"	14th		- do - do -	Excavation commenced for 6 Bomb Proof Shelters at N.12.d.3.8. Soup Kitchen at N.6.a.3.1. completed. Repairing CAMBRIA ROAD.
"	15th		- do - do -	Excavated for foundation for Concrete O.P. MONCHY.
"	16th		- do - do -	Bomb Proof Shelters at N.12.d.3.8. completed.
"	17th		- do - do -	Gas curtain frames in dug-outs completed.
"	18th		- do - do -	Excavation commenced for Cookhouse in EAST RESERVE. " " " " in VINE AVENUE. Gum Boot Store in ORANGE AVENUE completed
"	19th		- do - do -	Excavation commenced for Sock Changing Shed in ORCHARD RESERVE. Mile Track in MONCHY, 140 yards completed.
"	20th		- do - do -	
"	21st		- do - do -	
"	22nd		- do - do -	Two mine craters completed on CAMBRIA ROAD ready for seeling. Tramway at Crater Subway removed and laid in new position.
"	23rd		- do - do -	

A5814 Wt. W4973 M687 750,000 8/16 D. D. & L. Ltd. Forms/C.2118/13.

Army Form C. 2118.

WAR DIARY
or
INTELLIGENCE SUMMARY

(Erase heading not required.)

Instructions regarding War Diaries and Intelligence Summaries are contained in F. S. Regs., Part II. and the Staff Manual respectively. Title pages will be prepared in manuscript.

Place	Date	Hour	Summary of Events and Information	Remarks and references to Appendices
N.2.d.5.7.	24th.		Same as for 1st November. No.4 Section relieved No.1 Section on Forward work, No.1 Section took over work in ARRAS Area and moved to Billets in ARRAS.	
"	25th		- do - do - Repairing and cleaning Pumps in trenches in Sector.	
"	26th		- do - do -	
"	27th		- do - do - Roadmaking, SWORD LANE, 50 yards of road made up.	
"	28th		- do - do -	
"	29th		- do - do - Building Field Kitchens at SCHRAM BARRACKS, ARRAS commenced. Nos. 2 and 4 Sections relieved two Sections of 74th Field Company R.E. in new Sector and moved into billets at about H.36.a.1.4. Handed over work in old sector to Sections of 405th (Renfrew) Field Company R.E.	
"	30th		No.3 Section employed on O.P.s in MONCHY. Nos.2 and 4 Sections employed on repairing Decauville Track between B.403 Station and HAPPY VALLEY DUMP; Revetting and cleaning front line trench; Bunking in dug-outs in WELLFORD TRENCH and CURT SWITCH; Water Supply System - patrolling and general repairs.	
			Strength of Company on 30th November :- 7 Officers and 215 other ranks.	
			[signature] Major. R.E. O.C., 526th (Durham) Field Company R.E.	

War Diary
of
"The Officer Commanding, 526 (Durham) Field Co RE"
from 1st December to 31st December 1917.

WAR DIARY or INTELLIGENCE SUMMARY

Army Form C. 2118.

Place	Date	Hour	Summary of Events and Information	Remarks and references to Appendices
N.2.a.5.9. (Sy Huy:- Sheet 51.b. S.W.)	1/12/17		Casualties of Company 1st December 1917:- 7 Officers, 215 other ranks. Sections employed as follows:- No 1 Section, Billets in ARRAS, employed repairing etc BEAURAINS CAMP, Building Stables at SCHRAMM BARRACKS, Recovering roof of CAVALRY BARRACKS until dark fell. Section (Nos. 2 & 4) moved forward to HAPPY VALLEY (H.36.a.10.05 — Sheet 51.B. N.W.) No 2 Section stood - relieving No 3 Section of 74th Divisional Coy RE. No 3 Section employed Constructing 2 O.P.'s in MONCHY.	Lieut. R.E. Midwood still in hospital. Lieut. R.B. Williams still in hospital admitted to hospital.
"	2/12/17		Sections Nos 1 and 3 employed as on 1st December. " Section Nos 2 and 4 employed as follows in new area: Repairing and revetting front line shell at FORK 1 to 6 - Repairing & revetting Posts in Angle in ORANGE AVENUE and CURB SWITCH SOUTH - Repairing tramway from B40S sidings to HAPPY VALLEY DUMP (artillery) - Pulling water Pipe Line in Craters - Clearing & laying of Trench roads in BRIDOOX ALLEY. Company Headquarters and No 3 Section moved to HAPPY VALLEY.	
HAPPY VALLEY 3/12/19 (H.36.a.10.15) Pey Ply. 51.B. N.W.			No 3 Section employed as Above for 1st and 2nd in of. Except No 3 Section — Section devices new dirts on O.P.'s in MONCHY and Constructed Company mining conference	
"			to RESERVE LINE.	

WAR DIARY
or
INTELLIGENCE SUMMARY.
(Erase heading not required.)

Army Form C. 2118.

Instructions regarding War Diaries and Intelligence Summaries are contained in F. S. Regs., Part II. and the Staff Manual respectively. Title pages will be prepared in manuscript.

Place	Date	Hour	Summary of Events and Information	Remarks and references to Appendices
HAPPY VALLEY. (A 36 a.10.15) Sheet 51.B N.W.	4/9/19	—	Relief of Nos 1, 2 + 4 H. employed as previously stated. No 3 section commenced wiring RESERVE LINE — Arras Arras Senser.	
			HAPPY VALLEY in vicinity of Company Lines. No 4323 L/Cpl SMITH T. and Pte 54665 Capt. PRICE. H. admitted to Hospital sick. Casualties to Attached Infantry Party:- 1 OR Killed, 1 OR died of wounds, 2 wounded + 1 gassed.	
— " —	5/9/19 6/9/19		All sections employed as stated previously.	
— " —	7/9/19		Section Nos 1, 2 + 4, employed as stated. No 3 Section Completed wiring of RESERVE LINE. Wiring allotted to Company. Major WEIR proceeded to Lines of Communication Officers School at BLENDECQUES. & Capt. J.W. MORRIS took over temporary Command of Company.	
— " —	8/9/19		No 1 Section marched from ARRAS to HAPPY VALLEY and relieved No 3 Section in forward area. No 3 Section marched to ARRAS. Sections Nos 2 + 4 employed on work as previously stated.	
— " —	9/9/19		No 1 section commenced thickening wiring in front of WELFORD + BAYONET RESERVES. All section employed on wiring operations etc as stated.	

Army Form C. 2118.

WAR DIARY
or
INTELLIGENCE SUMMARY.
(Erase heading not required.)

Instructions regarding War Diaries and Intelligence Summaries are contained in F. S. Regs., Part II. and the Staff Manual respectively. Title pages will be prepared in manuscript.

Place	Date	Hour	Summary of Events and Information	Remarks and references to Appendices
HAPPY VALLEY. (A.36.a.10.15). Sh.57C N.W.	10/10/15		(a 2-0am) Orders received from Brigade No "Stand To" in position allotted in LIME AVENUE from 5-30 A.M. Then finish dug. before DISMISS. was received at 10-15 A.M. Section proceeded to work immediately after "Stand To" – deepening and finishing of SHAFFLE TRENCH – HALBERD TRENCH & RIFLE SUPPORT. Also not reporting 11-30 A.M. No.1 section leaving shelter on RESERVE LINE during at night. Sent R.G. Mibs discharged from hospital & proceeded on leave.	
" "	11/10/15		"Stand To" from 5-50 am to 10-0 am. w. – Section in LIME AVENUE reselled. Section employed as previously stated. No. 4 Section Comment. overhauling & repairing Emp. placed in August. In Section.	
" "	12/10/15		"Stand To" 6.0 a — 10" v.11" inch. Section employed on the at Over MARNE Lo.	
" "	13/10/15		Shelter finished.	
" "	14/10/15		"Stand To" cancelled. Section employed on usual overhauling. No.1 section commenced completing repair of Lewis Gun. Emplaced in WELFORD TRENCH – Also making Emplacement.	
" "	15/10/15		No.3 & No.1 R.19 Completed. Also completed at AID POST CUBE SWITCH SOUTH, 2/Lt. HERBERT to Hospital.	
" "	16/10/15		Section employed as previously stated – usual overhauling.	
" "	17/10/15		Section employed as stated. Also commenced on repair of 96 R.19 Commence.	

WAR DIARY or INTELLIGENCE SUMMARY

Army Form C. 2118.

Instructions regarding War Diaries and Intelligence Summaries are contained in F.S. Regs., Part II. and the Staff Manual respectively. Title pages will be prepared in manuscript.

(Erase heading not required.)

Place	Date	Hour	Summary of Events and Information	Remarks and references to Appendices
HAPPY VALLEY (H.36.a.10.15) Sheet 51.B.N.W.	18/9/16		1/5th Infy. resting in bivouac. Nos. 1 & 2 Section mostly Ration carrying as usual. Nos. 3 & 4 Section resting — Standby for Baths.	
" "	19/9/16		Maintenance of tracks continues — Section employed as previously stated.	
" "	20/9/16			
" "	21/9/16		Section employed as usual. Gunners as usual. Work continued on H.Cy. O.P.s R.S. & R.I.P. No.3 Section ordered forward for ARRAS & relieve No.2 Section in HAPPY VALLEY. No Infantry working parties available — 1/5th Section resting — Both Parties (Lift transport/Ds. — as usual)	
" "	22/9/16		Work continued on Grant tramway / Ginchin. Work commenced on Em. Road Appy. Shed in LONE AVENUE — "n" 23.4.9.19.	
" "	23/9/16			
" "	24/9/16		Lieutman. Ray. All Sections resting. 2nd/Lieut HERBERT returning from Hospital.	
" "	25/9/16		Additional work taken over from H.Cy. (Infy) "Ex. Drape in HIGHLAND" SUPPORT — "DALE TRENCH" & CHAIN SUPPORT. Section Enhances Sudans Overhead work.	
" "	27/9/16		1/5th Section Commenced work on Cornelgipen in front of WELFORD RESERVE. Maintenance work continues by old Section.	
" "	29/9/19		Section employed as previously stated. Work in Em. Road Shed LONE AVENUE Complete.	

Army Form C. 2118.

WAR DIARY
or
INTELLIGENCE SUMMARY.
(Erase heading not required.)

Instructions regarding War Diaries and Intelligence Summaries are contained in F.S. Regs., Part II. and the Staff Manual respectively. Title pages will be prepared in manuscript.

Place	Date	Hour	Summary of Events and Information	Remarks and references to Appendices
HAPPY VALLEY (H.26.c.10.15) (R.Shts. 51.B.N.W)	29/12/19		General routine work of trenches continued. 2nd Lieut. A.H. GADD proceeded to H.Q. on transfer to East Cors.	
" —	30/12/19		Major THWEIR – required for Senior Officers Course. Col. Keelin continues work on paragraphs 1 – 75% complete in front of MUSKET RESERVE and 1 – 60% complete in front of WELFORD RESERVE. 2nd Lt. HERBERT - member of study Ho. deputy dressing parties available – Keelin Nos. 3 & 4 reading – Buck Bridge. No 1 Keelin Captain & Paragraphs. No. 3 & 4.	
" —	30/12/19		Lieut. D.A. ROBERTS joined company from R.E. BASE. 2nd Lieut. W. HERBERT admitted to Hospital.	

Strength of Company 31st Dec. 1919 = 7 officers & 205 other ranks

(signed) J. Wright Lt.
a/c R.E.

J/6526 (Anstey)

4th Division

526th Field Company R.E.

January to December
1918

Jan - Feb. 1919

War Diary
of
The Officer Commanding 526th (Durham) Field Co RE.
from 1st January to 31st January 1918.

WAR DIARY or INTELLIGENCE SUMMARY.

Army Form C. 2118.

Instructions regarding War Diaries and Intelligence Summaries are contained in F.S. Regs., Part II. and the Staff Manual respectively. Title pages will be prepared in manuscript.

(Erase heading not required.)

Place	Date	Hour	Summary of Events and Information	Remarks and references to Appendices
HARRY VALLEY H 36 a 10.05. (Ref Sheet :- 51 B N.W.	1/1/18		Strength of Company 1st January 1918 :- 7 Officers, 204 O.R. Lectures employed in following units :- Dining in front of WELFORD RESERVE and MUSKET RESERVE, renewing of general maintenance of the following trenches, SHRAPNEL, HIGHLAND SUPPORT, MUSKET RESERVE, RIFLE SUPPORT, CHAIN SUPPORT, & CURB SWITCH NORTH, also draining DALE TRENCH AND CANISTER AVENUE, Patrolling water supply pipeline in trenches, Getting Dug Outs to Dugouts in Trenches.	
—	2/1/18		Work continues as stated for 1st inst.	
—	3/1/18		" "	
—	4/1/18		" "	
—	5/1/18		" "	
—	6/1/18		No. 1 Section relieved by No. 2 Section in forward area as stated.	
—	7/1/18			
—	8/1/18		Foot Bay. Inspection & Bath Parade. Lieut. J.W. HAYS joined from R.E. BASE. Lectures employed in renewing and erection of R.E. wire also fixing Repairs in dugouts, cleaning Sumps & distributing pumps, clearing up curly wire in SHRAPNEL TRENCH and front trenches in CHAYROOKS TRENCH.	
—	9/1/18		Dining trenches in front of SEABOARD SUPPORT, RIFLE SUPPORT, DALE TRENCH AND HIGHLAND SUPPORT — also work continues on general maintenance of trenches.	
—	10/1/18		Work continues as stated for 9th inst.	
—	11/1/18			

Army Form C. 2118.

WAR DIARY
or
INTELLIGENCE SUMMARY.
(Erase heading not required.)

Instructions regarding War Diaries and Intelligence Summaries are contained in F. S. Regs., Part II. and the Staff Manual respectively. Title pages will be prepared in manuscript.

Place	Date	Hour	Summary of Events and Information	Remarks and references to Appendices
HAPPY VALLEY H.36.a.10.05. (Ref: Sheet 57.B.N.W)	13/1/18		Work continues as division for B'mind. O.C. 1st Leicesters relieves O.C. 1st Georges in K trench. Capt. J.H. Harris takes no longer after Capt. J.H. Harris leave to UK tfc. — Capt. J.W. Harris leaves his company command of company. Major Evans proceeds to join 181st Tunnelling Company R.E. to be released for duty for Dunkirk.	
—	14/1/18		Work continues as above for B'mind.	
—	15/1/18			
—	16/1/18		Wiring & revetting employed to repair of Change Leicester Brigade — all station employed on dumping W & Clearing Leicester & laying of Duckboard tracks overland	
—	17/1/18			
—	18/1/18		The 3 Legion relieves the 1st Leicester in forward area. No. 2000 91 Coppr. Williams from No. 471490 Coppr. Rowley & number 19/11/18. Reporting on & Clearing of trench Contined. also laying of Duckboard tracks under taken completed. No. 470302 Coppr. McDonald to number 201/1/18.	
—	20/1/18 21/1/18		Section employed preparing revetting materials & improving country of some up to trenches.	
—	22/1/18		Relaying & revetting the following trenches: RIFLE SUPPORT — DALE TRENCH — HIGHLAND SUPPORT — CHAIN SUPPORT. Pump gulleries & pumping dugouts. Clearing trenches & forming at night.	
—	23/1/18 24/1/18			

T2131. Wt. W708-776. 500,000. 4/15. Sir J. C. & S.

Army Form C. 2118.

WAR DIARY
or
INTELLIGENCE SUMMARY.
(Erase heading not required.)

Instructions regarding War Diaries and Intelligence Summaries are contained in F. S. Regs., Part II and the Staff Manual respectively. Title Pages will be prepared in manuscript.

Place	Date	Hour	Summary of Events and Information	Remarks and references to Appendices
HAPPY VALLEY H.36.a.10.05 (Ref Sheet 51 B N.W)	28/1/18		Ant. Continues on extension of 23" road. Lieut. E.J. Green, 2nd Pioneer of Wellington Regt. attached to Company 28/1/18.	
	29/1/18		Major H.H. Ythu returned from leave 29/1/18.	
	29/1/18		Lieut. J.G. Gatty returned to 161st Tunnelling Eng. RE. 29/1/18.	
	29/1/18		Large Infantry Parties (2 Battalions) employed with R.E. Engineers clearing communication trenches, cleaning dugouts etc. — from 29th inst onwards.	
	31/1/18		Strength of Company 31st January 1918 :— 10 Officers & 194 O.R.	

J. W. W Wegener
Major
O 505 Commander T. Coy RE

526 4A Copy RG

Army Form C. 2118.

WAR DIARY
or
INTELLIGENCE SUMMARY
(Erase heading not required)

Instructions regarding War Diaries and Intelligence Summaries are contained in F.S. Regs., Part II and the Staff Manual respectively. Title pages will be prepared in manuscript.

Place	Date	Hour	Summary of Events and Information	Remarks and references to Appendices
HAPPY VALLEY H.36.a.10.05 Ref. Sheet 51 B N.W.	1/2/18		Strength of Company on 1/2/18:- 7 Officers 170 O.R. Parks. Lectures on types of Leaders. Cleaning Livres/Digging chain & relaying the chain on Knolls in the Infantry trenches. RIFLE SUPPORT - CHAIN SUPPORT of HIGHLAND SUPPORT. Cleaning Opens Back of ORANGE AVENUE & widening, Cleaning & relaying CHAIN SUPPORT and RIFLE SUPPORT to large infantry posts, mail RE Craterium. Taking dead horses to Army dump in rear. Water supply parties. Craterium for rail line & wire at WELFORD RESERVE.	
-"-	2/2/18		Cleaning & relaying Digging chain & relaying trenches in RIFLE "CHAIN SUPPORTS Cleaning Burns in LONG AVENUE by 3rd Infantry. Working party wiring RE Craterium. Laying down drains. Water Supply parties. Craterium for new Tipline at WELFORD.	
-"-	3/2/18 4/2/18		Deleted employed on work as described for 1st, 2nd, & 3rd.	
SCHRAMM BARRACKS ARRAS	5/2/18		Company Officers from HAPPY VALLEY to SCHRAMM BARRACKS - relieved by 74th (?) Division Company RE of 15th Division.	
-"-	6/2/18		Inspection of Gas Shelter & Officer air defense. Company uniform readers. Bath Parade.	
-"-	7/2/18		Inspection & reading of such equipment. Lectures on Demolitions, Lewisian Demolition, Lewis Drill, Rifle Exercises, Gas Drill.	
-"-	8/2/18		Truck, Camps, Use of Spies, Types of Bridges, Drivers, of the staff etc. Lewis Gunnery, Map reading, Use of Company, New Pfds to 11th Infantry or detachment.	
-"-	9/2/18 10/2/18		Company inspection by G.O.C. in Line Marching Order. Fire Day. Church Parades. Capt. Jas. Norris proceeded Leave.	

(35091) Wt. W12590/M1293. 75,000. 1/17. D.D. & L., Ltd. Forms/C2118/14.

Army Form C. 2118.

WAR DIARY
or
INTELLIGENCE SUMMARY.
(Erase heading not required.)

Instructions regarding War Diaries and Intelligence Summaries are contained in F. S. Regs., Part II. and the Staff Manual respectively. Title pages will be prepared in manuscript.

Place	Date	Hour	Summary of Events and Information	Remarks and references to Appendices
SCHRAMM BARRACKS	11/2/18		Company Drill. Cleaning equipment.	
ARRAS.	12/2/18		Company Drill. Lecture on duties for 8/2/18. also Lecture to Officers and N.C.O. on Lewis Gun.	
"	13/2/18		Company Drill. Cleaning equipment.	
"	14/2/18		Inspection by O/C. Hanging Fatigue - Cleaning wagons. Lecture to N.C.O.s on school over Lines Mysking Order.	
"	15/2/18		Parties of Officers & men inspected by G.O.C. + Division in afternoon.	
ARRAS.	16/2/18		Company moved from SCHRAMM BARRACKS to No 28 RUE FREDERIC DE GEORGE. ARRAS. Lieut H. J. Foster left unit for 18 ltd. Sanmillary Coy. R.E. (unemployed)	
"	17/2/18 18/2/18		Sections erecting target wire defences around LES FOSSES FARM. N.12.a N.2c. N.11.c.9.1 N10. 3-8339 Sapper Widey "Wounded in Action"	
"	19/2/18 20/2/18		Work as detailed for 17"×18" instant and sleeping trench for two dugouts at ORANGE HILL H.34. 6.6.4. 1 OR reinforcement joined by from Release Depot.	
"	21/2/18		Works detailed for 17 × 18 instant. Commenced to drive shafts to two dugouts at ORANGE HILL H.34. 6.6.4. (Sht 51.B.NW) Lieut J.W. Mays "Wounded in Action"	

WAR DIARY or INTELLIGENCE SUMMARY

Army Form C. 2118.

Place	Date	Hour	Summary of Events and Information	Remarks and references to Appendices
ARRAS	22/9/18		Wiring as detailed for 17 & 18 instant. Excavating and greeting frames in entrances to two dugouts ORANGE HILL H.34.d.3.4. 1 O.R. proceeded to U.K. from 9 Field Coy R.E.	
"	23/9/18		Work as detailed for 22nd instant. 2/Lieut A.J. Endling joined unit from 77 Field Coy R.E.	
"	24/9/18		Rest Day. Inspection of Arms & Equipment took back deployed and deficiencies taken. Received an Lewis Gun from Ordnance for use at Company Transport Lines against hostile Aircraft.	
"	25/9/18		Wiring as detailed for 17 & 18 instant. Erecting frames in entrances to dugouts ORANGE HILL H.34.d.3.4. Commenced work on two dugouts in BROWN LINE N.10.d.3.8. (Sketch 51 R.S.W.) N° 47104 & Sapper McGhee W. wounded on Action. 3 O.Rs. joined unit from R.E. Base Depot. 1 Officer + 3 Groups of Infantry attached to Coy for work in dugouts.	
"	26/9/18		Wiring as detailed for 17 & 18 instant. Erecting frames in entrances to two dugouts at ORANGE HILL H.34.d.6.4. and two dugouts in BROWN LINE N.10.d.3.6. Lieut J.W. Morris rejoins Coy from leave.	
"	27/9/18 28/9/18		Work as detailed for 26 instant.	

Company strength 6 Officers 196 O.R.

J.W. West Major R.E.
O.C. 526 (Durham) Fd. Co. R.E.

4th Div.

WAR DIARY

526th (DURHAM) FIELD COMPANY, R.E.

M A R C H

1 9 1 8

War Diary

of

The Officer Commanding 526th (Durham) Field Co. R.E.

from 1st March to 31st March 1918.

Army Form C. 2118.

WAR DIARY
or
INTELLIGENCE SUMMARY.
(Erase heading not required.)

Place	Date	Hour	Summary of Events and Information	Remarks and references to Appendices
ARRAS	1/3/18		Strength of Company on 1/3/18 :- 6 Officers 193 Other ranks. 2nd Lieut. A HUGHES joined Coy on 1.3.18. Sections employed on excavation of 2 Dugouts in ORANGE HILL at H.34.a.9.5 & H.34.a.9.7. and 2 Dugouts in BROWN LINE at N.10.a.8.3 & N.10.a.8.1 - also entrance to east Dugout. Also employed in laying wire Entanglement in front of BROWN LINE at about N.4.a.9.0. throughout.	
" "	2/3/18		Rest Day. Instructions etc.	
" "	3/3/18		Lecture to Heavy Artillery Officers on Entanglements & Construction of Double Apron Fence, Knife Rest Entanglements and by Officers and N.C.Os. on Entanglements. (Lecture repeated on Lieut.(?))	
" "	4/3/18		Sections employed on works in Divis. area etc. 10.0.6.a.m.	
" "	5/3/18		Lecture to all ranks on 5" Mortar on Enemy's Sabotage.	
" "	6/3/18		Sections employed on Dug.ing & wire Entanglement as previously ordered.	
" "	7/3/18		Battalion given up all works on Sulphur Lane. Details in hands of 2 Section with Rest Centre.	
" "	8/3/18		Orchard. Alarm Scheme - Stand turn out :- Alarm Whistles previous warning given at 4.30 a.m.	
" "	9/3/18		When Gas Alert. Driven without assistance of Officers turned up all Others at 4:45 a.m. and 2 Teams from alarm being given, first went, Instructions etc.	
" "	10/3/18		Rest day. Instructions etc.	
" "	11/3/18		Sections employed on Dug.ing & wire Entanglement as previously ordered. Box Respirators Drills continue.	
" "	12/3/18		Warning Order received by Company to be ready to leave at date of advance from 5.0. a.m. at 4.30 a.m. - all Orderlies packed & Company ready to leave at notice & arrive at 5.0 a.m.	
" "	13/3/18		Sections employed on works at usual sites.	
" "	14/3/18		Sections employed on Dug.ing & wire Entanglement. Lect. "Cap." Signs Gases on wire. Lecture by Section Officers to Sections on Lines Economy in relation to Dug.ing etc.	

Army Form C. 2118.

WAR DIARY
or
INTELLIGENCE SUMMARY.
(Erase heading not required.)

Instructions regarding War Diaries and Intelligence Summaries are contained in F. S. Regs., Part II. and the Staff Manual respectively. Title pages will be prepared in manuscript.

Place	Date	Hour	Summary of Events and Information	Remarks and references to Appendices
ARRAS	15/3/18		Sections employed in Dug out & Wire Entanglement.	
--	16/3/18		All ranks paraded though Gas Chamber & had Box Respirators tested by Divisional Gas Officer on 16th inst.	
--	17/3/18		Rest Day. Inspection use.	
--	18/3/18		Sections employed in Dug out & Wire Entanglement.	
--	19/3/18			
--	20/3/18		Casualties of 2nd March:- No 470086 L/Cpl. R.K. PARKER. Gassed ; No 470893 L/Cpl. DICKSON G.A. WOUNDED. Gassed (Since died of wounds). No 550170 Capt DRAKE. H. – No 470840 Capt FLANAGAN. A. – and No 536160 Capt STANDING R.A. – Gassed.	
--	21/3/18			
STIRLING CAMP. H.13.d.7.8.	22/3/18		Company moved from ARRAS to STIRLING CAMP (H.13.d.7.8). Sections moved from ARRAS to ST. NICHOLAS (S.16.a.5.7). No 1 & 2 Sections proceeded forward to Bridges in H.23. Central. 2 Sub-M. Swares left in Charge of Demolition of Bridges at H.18.a.2.1, H.2d.a.5.7, H.2d.a.6.6, H.2d. Central, H.23.a.9.4, and H.28.a.9.9.	
ETRUN.	23/3/18		Company moved from STIRLING CAMP to ETRUN. Sections marched at 3-30 A.M to move at 4-40 A.M from ST. NICHOLAS to L.17.a. in the ST. POL Road and in the afternoon to ETRUN. Lieut RE. MILES Constructed Pontoon Bridge over R. SCARPE and then rejoined Company at ETRUN. Party left at H.23. Central to maintain Pontoon Bridge. Casualties for 23rd inst:- No. 471179 L/Corp MURRAY T. wounded. 2nd Lieut A. HUGHES and No 410334 Sergt. BROCKBANK. F. evacuated to N. Army Schools of Instruction. Company employed in preparing Defensive Line (Purple Line) Lane of DAINVILLE. Digging and Wiring.	
--	24/3/18		2nd Lieut N. SWARES, in Charge of demolition party, Wounded, and No 470822 L/Cpl Kay L/Cpl BERSHAW. N and No 470943 Sapper DOBSON. M. wounded, by Enemy Snipers. No 470822 L/Cpl Kay L/Cpl A.J. CODLING Sent out missing. 2nd Lieut	

Army Form C. 2118.

WAR DIARY
or
INTELLIGENCE SUMMARY.

(Erase heading not required.)

Instructions regarding War Diaries and Intelligence Summaries are contained in F.S. Regs., Part II. and the Staff Manual respectively. Title pages will be prepared in manuscript.

Place	Date	Hour	Summary of Events and Information	Remarks and references to Appendices
ETRUN.	23/3/18		Company employed in preparing defensive line (Purple Line) East of DAINVILLE — digging and wiring. Lieut. D.A. ROBERTS reported to 11th Infantry Brigade.	
" "	24/3/18		Company employed as for 23rd inst.	
" "	27/3/18		Company employed as for 23rd inst. Charges laid for Demolition of two bridges at ATHIES LOCK (H.24.a.3.7.). Work employed by 5 P.M. Lieut. R.E. MILES and party in charge of these two bridges and old German bridge at H.22.a.7.3. No. 140262 2nd/Corpl MOURSE. G. volunteered.	
	28/3/18		Cpl. Leary change the German Alliance Divisions front. Euripe Cross Bridge (H.18.d.2d.) Lupte Cross Bridge (H.24.a.5.7.); Wooden Bridge (H.24.a.6.6.); Enlass Bridge (H.24.a.8.); 2 Bridges at FAMPOUX LOCK (H.23 a.7.7.; M.23 a.7.7.) Discharged by 2nd Lieut. A.T. GODWIN. in the morning. Two bridges at ATHIES LOCK (H.21.a.3.7.) and wooden bridge over SCARPE (H.22.a.7.3.) destroyed by Lieut. R.E. MILES late in the afternoon. 4 Sections of Company moved at 8.0 A.M. from ETRUN to the MOAT, ARRAS. During the morning the Company lined the old 2 Companies of the Division overran the Army line wanted in front of factory from the R. SCARPE to 500 yds North of GAVRELLE ROAD. Telephone lifted the Line between H.14. c.o.o. to H.8. a. 4.3. Late in morning Company marched forward to near MISSOURI Trench. Return in the eng., 9th the Coy in Cable, and 4 Sec (Sapper) staffs on right. Company arrived at 8.0 P.M. and marched back to STARLING CAMP.	
			Casualties for 28th inst:— No. 457.847. Cpl. GLADDERS. W. Killed.
			Cpl. 470.093 Sapper TOOLEY. T.E. Wounded. (Since died).
			Cpl. 470.721 Sapper SMITH. R. "
			Cpl. 470.248 " ROBSON. T.H. "
			Cpl. 459.584 " SCOTT. J.W. "
			Cpl. 470.258 " LIDDELL. W.F. "
			Cpl. 506110 Spmr WHITTAKER. A. " (R.A.M.C. attached).

Army Form C. 2118.

WAR DIARY
or
INTELLIGENCE SUMMARY.
(Erase heading not required)

Instructions regarding War Diaries and Intelligence Summaries are contained in F. S. Regs., Part II. and the Staff Manual respectively. Title pages will be prepared in manuscript.

Place	Date	Hour	Summary of Events and Information	Remarks and references to Appendices
STIRLING Camp. H.13.a.7.8.	29/3/18	11-0 P.M.	Company ordered to man EFFIE TRENCH (H.16.a.3.6 to H.9.a.2.7.) at 11-0 P.M. Garrison on the left, 9" Hay on the right.	
— " —	30/3/18.		Company in EFFIE TRENCH. Lieut. R.E. MILES and 2nd Lieut. A.J. CODLING rejoined from ETRUN.	
— " —	31/3/18.		Company relieved in EFFIE TRENCH at 6-0 A.M. by 2nd West Rides (Pioneers) and returned to STIRLING Camp. 2nd Lieut. A.J. CODLING laying charges on two bridges at BLANGY LOCK and in charge of scheme for making a crater at H.19.d. & d.6. Company worked in the afternoon on Intermediate Army Line East of BLANGY LOCK, improving trench running between SCARPE and FAMPOUX ROAD. G.18.a. Central. Casualties for 31 minutes Cpl. 47069 O. 2/Corpl. WEBSTER. F. wounded.	

Strength of Company on 31st March 1918 :- 6 Officers & 193 other ranks.

J. West
Major R.E.
O.C. 526 (Durham) Field Coy. R.E.

(A7092) Wt W12939/M1293. 75,000. 1/17. D.D. & L., Ltd. Forms/C.2118/14.

4th Divisional Engineers

526th (Durham) FIELD COMPANY R. E.

APRIL 1918.

War Diary
of
"The Officer Commanding 526th (Durham) Field Company R.E."
From 1st April to 30th April 1918

WAR DIARY
or
INTELLIGENCE SUMMARY.
(Erase heading not required.)

Army Form C. 2118.

526 I.C.R.E.

Place	Date	Hour	Summary of Events and Information	Remarks and references to Appendices
STARLING CAMP	1/4/18		Strength of Company in Field :- 6 Officers 193 other ranks.	
H.13.c.9.2 (Sheet 51.B N.W.)	2/4/18		Section Employ'd in Delivering One Line East of BLANGY. Loct— improving Street between River SCARPE and FAMPOUX ROAD (C.'s & a. Central) Wired cabling party in charge of Clearing Charges at BLANGY Loop Bridge and mine firing cable at H.19 & 4.6. Casualties for 1 mo :- 401242 Sapper Dean C. wounded. " 2 " :- 470 326 W/cpl Watson T. wounded (at duty).	
ST LAURENT BLANGY. G.18.c.5.U.	3/4/18	5 AM	Reconnoisance by Captain Enteakinshank assisted by 2nd Lieut Hayton & Lieut Brackely improving tht front of ST LAURENT BLANGY (in cellar) School. Section employed on work as indicated for 12", 2nd mo.	
"	4/4/18			
"	5/4/18		Company of Engineers Charge as above. Reinforcements from H.10.a.9.6 to H.9.a.9.7. on 3/4/18 Took over + 150 ors of 1/10 Leinster Loyalist Battalion assigned to various advance trenches. No.1 Section complete as in 3" mo st. No. 2, 3, + 4 Section complete as above. No 490287 Sapper Coron J, 490939 Sapper Adams, 401123 Sapper Officers W. Army 189763 Sapper Berry Jas. Answered the Muster posted.	
"	6/4/18		Work as above for 5" mo.	
"	7/4/18		— do —	
Y"Harane J. L.1.a.9.6. (Sheet 51 SW.E)	8/4/18		Reconnaisance Section by Engineers moves from ST LAURENT BLANGY to Y"Harane J. Personnel Section moved from ETRUN to Y" Harane J.	
	9/4/18		Intercede: School v La Quivo.	
HAUTE AVESNES	10/4/18		Company moves from Y"Haraune J. to HAUTE AVESNES. 40 Stationary & Garrison Company.	

WAR DIARY
or
INTELLIGENCE SUMMARY.

(Erase heading not required.)

Army Form C. 2118.

Instructions regarding War Diaries and Intelligence Summaries are contained in F. S. Regs., Part II. and the Staff Manual respectively. Title pages will be prepared in manuscript.

Place	Date	Hour	Summary of Events and Information	Remarks and references to Appendices
HAUTE AVESNES	11/4/18		Working & Inspecting Gas Drills. Orders received from CoRE + Division + Headquarters 11th Tank Brigade to be prepared to move at short notice. 2nd Lieut A.J. CODLING arrived RE Mess and 2nd Lieut A.J. CODLING arrived the Wilding Bros.	
LE HAMEL	12/4/18		Company Section marched to "Y" Battn H.Q. + moved by Bus from there to LILLERS – thence by march route to LE HAMEL. Mannten Section moved by march route. Company on Inspection &c.	
	13/4/18			
CHATEAU de-WERPPE W.19.a.7.2	14/4/18		Company Section moved from LE HAMEL to CHATEAU – de – WERPPE at W.19.a.7.2. Mannten in Aeroplane Hangar. Lieut Tobin & one party one 2nd Lieut Stanghs + party (Demolition parties) took Bridges at P.29.c.6.2. – P.36.a.2.6. Q.31.a.7.2. Q.32.c.6.9. Held Supply line close up – working party of 2 Companies Pioneers digging (?)	
—	15/4/18		Section employees wiring in front of our support line. 1 Sey Pioneer digging. Alternate of Demolition Charges at Bridges – No 518591 Seyt J Dennis J.A. Killed No 521384 Copt Ponds was one No 281959 Capt Ander Lt wounded 17/4/18.	
—	16/4/18			
—	17/4/18			
—	18/4/18		Warning Orders received overnight 17/1/18 in event of probable enemy attack. Demolition parties warned to stand to "to blow up bridges if necessary. Company "Standing to" from 5.0am. until 8.30am. Select Bridge at Q.32.c.6.9. Aleroniere at 6am. (Crossed by Infantry Bridges continues. Renewal of Company employees wiring & dug supports line. 2nd Lieut J.S. ESMC HARDY joined Company from R.E. Base.	

(A7092) Wt.W21999/M1293. 75,000. 1/17. D.D. & L. Ltd. Forms/C2118/14.

WAR DIARY
or
INTELLIGENCE SUMMARY.

(Erase heading not required.)

Army Form C. 2118.

Place	Date	Hour	Summary of Events and Information	Remarks and references to Appendices
CHATEAU DE WAYRIN W.19.a.9.2.	19/4/18		Kinking Henderson Charges at 3 rendering Bridges - Employees Classified of Bridges at P.32.C.6.9. Between Food Bridge across Canal at Q.32.C.6.9. Wiring Entrance of Keel Support Line.	
" "	20/4/18		Reconnre Henderson Charges. Wiring Entrance of Keel Support Line. Reconnre M.G. Emplacements Omn. Sec. or average at W.3.C.2.6.	
" "	21/4/18		Classified of Henderson Charge. No.3 Bridge at Q.31.a.9.2. destroyed by enemy shell fire. Barge for Bridge ordered to replace same. Wiring Keel Support Line. Ordered M.G. Emplacements at W.8.C.2.6. receives direct hit by shell at 9 p.m. and the whole being demolished, rendering further work impossible. Casualties (to 24 mid.) No 16201 Enzystoms, Lieut: T.S. Killed. " 471111 " Mape. " " " 470336 " Delarge. J " " " 164979 " Strangwood " Wounded. " 616646 " Green " " " 551139 " Ackenley A " " " 540390 " Bowl J.a. " " " " Denzipa "	
" "	22/4/18		"Wiring to" from 5 am. until 9-30 am. Keel Bridge So. P.29.C.C.2. Register an to 61st Division Wiring Keel Support Line. Ventaining of remaining Bridges. Casualties for 25 mid. No. 406098 Cpl: Barnely T.V. (Severe) " 126292 " Ackenton M. (Minor)	
" "	23/4/18		"Wire to" from 5 am to 9-30 am. Keplaining of Henderson Charges or Brune Cromote on Bridges. Wiring Keel Support Line. Captain W.G. Enthorne Commr. Gen. at W.&.C.9.8.	

Army Form C. 2118.

WAR DIARY
or
INTELLIGENCE SUMMARY.
(Erase heading not required)

Instructions regarding War Diaries and Intelligence Summaries are contained in F. S. Regs., Part II. and the Staff Manual respectively. Title pages will be prepared in manuscript.

Place	Date	Hour	Summary of Events and Information	Remarks and references to Appendices
CHATEAU de WERPPE W.19.a.7.7.	24/4/18		Various Reconn. Parties in Bernenchon Chures. Commenced + Completed 2 Chupes Fireplaces for M.G.C. near Enf. BERNENCHON Chures. Work continued on Evidence M.G. Emplacement at W.6.d.9.8.	
	25/4/18		Bridge Recce over R. 406" (Repaid Field Coy R.E. Wining of Support line. Erected M.G. Emplacement. Carrying trench through BOIS - de - PACAUT. Casualties for 25/4/18 :- 2/470821 Sapp. Jackson G Killed. 2/457687 " " Chuffield D. Wounded	
	26/4/18		Work continued on M.G. Emplacement. Clearing Broutrons and creating Breastworks in BOIS - de - PACAUT.	
V.23.a.0.9. (near LENGLET)	27/4/18		Company Headquarters + Dismountable section moved to V.23.a.0.9. Work continued as stated for 27/4/18.	
	28/4/18		Work continued on Enemies M.G. Emplacement & Breastworks in BOIS - de - PACAUT. Creating in + repairing digging of G.F.Q. in vicinity of BOIS - de - PACAUT.	
	29/4/18		Work on Enemies M.G. Emplacement & Breastworks continued. Improving wiring of F.O.P. in N.E. of BOIS - de - PACAUT. Casualties for 30/4/18:- 2/519267 Sapp. Hoskins L. Killed. " " 204136 " Bates Z. Wounded.	
	30/4/18		Strength of Company on 30th inst:- 7 Officers + 190 other ranks.	

[Signature]
Maguire
Major R.E.
O/c 526 (Durham) Field Company R.E.

War Diary

of

The Officer Commanding 526th (Durham) Field Company R.E.

from 1st May to 31st May 1918.

WAR DIARY or INTELLIGENCE SUMMARY

Army Form C. 2118.

Place	Date	Hour	Summary of Events and Information	Remarks and references to Appendices
Sheet 36A. V.23.c.0.9.	1/5/18		Company strength 1st May 1918:- 7 Officers + 190 other ranks. Company continues on Tunnels N.S. Emplacements at W.24.d.9.8. and Breastworks in Bois du Preaut. Excavation commenced for Body Elephant Shelter between Q.32.a. and W.3.t. Using half copper for same. Also Breastworks between Q.26.a.3.3. & Q.33.c.60.85.	
	2/5/18		Work continues on Tunnels N.S. Emplacements, Breastworks & Body Elephant Shelter as already for 1st inst.	
	3/5/18		Three N.C.O's & Reporting disc. of the Corps Tr. on decision for 1 point Auxiliary Equip. Left Battalion are relieving. One firing Gas Drum winners at W.3.a. Lys Brigade. On delivery for 2" inst.	
	4/5/18		Work continues on N.S. Emplacements, Breastworks & Body Elephant. Commenced Elephant Shelter at W.2.t.4.4. + W.I.a.35.55. + 12" Brigade HQ. Assisting R.E. Brigade wiring.	
	5/5/18		Same as above for 4th inst. N.S. Emplacements Complete as listed.	
	6/5/18		Short slope for 96rs Elephant line between Q.33.a.52. to W.m.a.6. at + losing tape for same.	
	7/5/18		Out not from Q.33.a.6.3 to Q.32.t.6.5 on Tunnel. Lieut. J.S. MacHardy evacuated to R.E. Base on Tunnel.	
	8/5/18		Work continues on Breastworks, Body Elephant & Elephant Shelter. Evacuation tapping of Spelling at 12" Divn Ambulance at V.26.d.7.8. 600 ft. Duckboard Shed lines Complete on Camp Bank in W.3.t. Casualties:- Major. T.H. Weir. Killed in Action. 8/5/18. " " Capt. Middleton. " " " " " PE 471327 Lance Cpl Anderson " " " "	
	9/5/18		Work continues on Breastworks & Elephant Shelter. Body Elephant between Q.32.a.and W.3.t. Complete. Specimen tapping of Spelling at V.26.d.0.8.	

WAR DIARY
or
INTELLIGENCE SUMMARY.

Army Form C. 2118.

Place	Date	Hour	Summary of Events and Information	Remarks and references to Appendices
SHEET 36A V.23.a.0.4.	10/5/16		Wire entanglement Brooklyn trench at V.26.d.7.8. Strong point at M.S. Pillbox at W.8.t.7.8. Gapping from W.B.T. 95.60 & W.3.c.7.9. Enemies fire heavy.	
— —	11/5/16		Not W.t.a. 6.5. (a 11" find). Same as above. 10" find.	
— —	10/5/16		Desultory shrapnel & H.E. shells over W144.8.9.2 & W 114.a.9.7. on entrance A.E. [illegible] take tolls for strong pillbox Q.33 a. 9.3	
— —	13/5/16		200 Lowther Queen Cross snipers in W.t.a. 8 and 12" find. Searching for 12" find. The Moose Wells BATTLE B. Sheen in Gas. M.G. 43.t.341 Number T.5 bombers.	
BUSNETTES 14/5/16.			Company ordered to BUSNETTES. Wire down in bivouac pits. 11", 12" & 13" find.	
— —	15/5/16		Capt. J.W. NORRIS. RE. assumed command of company with effect from 9th May 1916 and 2nd Lieut. E. INGLEBY struck from 10.6" (Right) Lieut 2nd Lt. INGLEBY vacated position of 2nd in command will take effect from 13th May 1916. Companies evacuating for Cape Helles shell at Anson brigade trenches. Also & Lieut. Kipling at M.G. Enfiled at W.B. & 9.8. between 6 Buxancent & Arwylordin Round at V.2.a. & B.B between Camomiles. Work continue at Lepper Street at W.B.Z.4.4. & Right Bale co-in. charges served at Bivouac. Infantry ordered infantry working trenches.	
— —	16/5/16		Wiring in Q.33.a. 9.9 and (Capital Test).	
— —	31/5/16		Work continued as for 15th inst.	

Army Form C. 2118.

WAR DIARY
or
INTELLIGENCE SUMMARY.
(Erase heading not required.)

Instructions regarding War Diaries and Intelligence Summaries are contained in F.S. Regs., Part II. and the Staff Manual respectively. Title pages will be prepared in manuscript.

Place	Date	Hour	Summary of Events and Information	Remarks and references to Appendices
BUSNETTES	18/5/18		Work continues at Aire Rue Keep & steel at W.2.b.4.4. & Rifle Pits. Wire Entanglements, Coy HQ Banks in W.3.d. Kemmel.	
	19/5/18		Work continues on 33 Shelters & M.G. Emplacements at W.8.t. 9.8. Twenty Bustard Breastworks & transport lines Copies forward to steel & covered works in support line.	
	20/5/18		Work continues as W.3.e.9.8. (20 mas)	
	21/5/18		Work continues on shelters for 16", 19" & 20" wiring Bank in Q.33.d. & W.H.d.2. – 2nd Reef Supper Line – also covering open trench in Canal Bank in Q.33.c. & W.3.a.v.t.	
	27/5/18		Work continues in Aire Rue Keep, Steel at W.2.b.4.4. Rifle Pits Keep & Breastworks, Transport lines – also turning Wire Q.33.d. & W.H.a.3 & Maintenance Trellis in Q.32.c. & W.3.d.4. Steel covers at Emily Keep in Q.33.a.O.3. & Q.33.d. 6.3.	
	25/5/18		Charges removed from Bridges at V.14.a.9.7. & V.14.c.9.2. & 23/5/18.	
	26/5/18		Cassantis – 29/5/18. No 40726. 2/Corps BARKER A.E. Leave on Return.	
	29/5/18		Wiring & Shelter Keep laffat lone Emplacements & Wire in Coma Park in Q.33. & W.3 & v.R. Front Col Bar at M.G. Emplacements at W.6.t.9.6. Indicating Inf. in Wiring. Work continues at Emily Rue Keep, Lidey Steel Coppies at Q.33. C.5.9. (Lidgel D) covering keep at Coy HQ in McGregor & Steel at W.2.b.4.4. Riffle Blue Evacuated as BUSNETTES.	
	30/5/18		Work continues on shelters for 25" & Also Emplacements for evacuee 2 steel at Q.33.d.2.t. – on at Q.33. C.5.9. and in Q.33.a.O.3. Also Lidgel for Clue & Driving Station at W.2.a.7.2.	
	27/5/18 28/5/18			
	29/5/18 30/5/18		Work continues on Officer Rest Quarters, Ruet Kops at W.2.b.4.4. Maintenance Trellis W.3.c.7.8. to W.3.d.3c. and W.3.c.3.3. to W.3.a.7.1. Aire Rue Keep. Coy Emplacements of M.G. Emplacements W.6.t.9.6. Maintenance Rest store & SAA Store Completed on Charcel Forest in V.16.c. Lewis Pulses Boards Placed in	

Army Form C. 2118.

WAR DIARY
or
INTELLIGENCE SUMMARY.
(Erase heading not required)

Place	Date	Hour	Summary of Events and Information	Remarks and references to Appendices
BUSNETTES.	31/5/18	(Contd.)	1st, 2nd, 4th Reserve Lines & 2nd Systems Front & Support Line. Repairing Posts in Reserve Line. 3 new Shelter frames complete in support line in Q 33 a. 1 new Shelter frame complete at entrance to Coy H.Q. in support line at Q 33 a. 3.1. 2 new standards or struts in support line in Q 33 a. Laying & fixing new Rifle of Horse shoe support in W 33 d. & Q 33 d. Continuing excavation for shelter in company H.Q. at Q 33. a. 9 5. Revetting dugout in eating.	
	31/5/18		Work on Reserve Line 20 md. Captain E.T. INGLEBY proceeded to Veterinary Course at NEUF-CHATEL. 6 Officers & 241 other ranks. Company strengths at 31/5/18.	

T. Ingleby
O.C. 526 (Durham) Field Company R.E.

War Diary
of
The Officer Commanding 526th (Durham) Field Company R.E.

From 1st June to 30th June 1918.

Army Form C. 2118.

WAR DIARY
or
INTELLIGENCE SUMMARY.
(Erase heading not required.)

Instructions regarding War Diaries and Intelligence Summaries are contained in F.S. Regs, Part II. and the Staff Manual respectively. Title pages will be prepared in manuscript.

Place	Date	Hour	Summary of Events and Information	Remarks and references to Appendices
BUSNETTES			Strength of Company 1st June 1918:- 6 Officers 211 other ranks.	
	1/6/18		Section employed as follows:- Erecting Officers Baths at BUSNETTES v laying Duckboards in Horse Baths at BUSNETTES.	
—	2/6/18		Work continued as above. Eating 5o Curtain at W.2.4. & I. Fr. Bort. H.Qrs. also Cable at W.8. a. 1.9. Ft. Arm. Bde. H.Qrs.	
—	3/6/18		Work continued as above. Laying trench tramway in support line. Infantry. Calso Canal Bank & repairing wire between Q.32.a. 3.2 v W.2.& b. 4.5. Infantry in Wiring.	
—	4/6/18		Officers Baths at BUSNETTES completed. Reminder of work as duties for 1st. Continued.	
—	5/6/18		Also repairing extension of Baths at W.8.a.1.9. Field Ambulance - Extending Pte. Light line there & Aven Bde Hd. at W.8.a.1.9. for Fort Aire Rd. - Enemy gas and shelling.	
—	6/6/18			
—	7/6/18			
—	8/6/18		Sections employed as stated above, also Preparing Bridge at V.13.a.7.9 for repairs.	
—	9/6/18		Work continued in East Hd. at W.2.& 4. 1, Aven Bde Hd. at W.8.a.1.9., Bath at 1st Field Ambulance, Ford v Canal Bank, Sleepers in Support Line & Knightsbridge. Repair Bridge at V.13.a.7.9. Also taking down fine 2" Duckbrn. & Widening by 12" v taking	
—	10/6/18		sliding Gas Alarms at Coy. Hd. at Q.32.a. 6.9 & 12 mins.	
—	11/6/18			
—	12/6/18			
—	13/6/18		Sections employed on work as outlined above, for 9" trench mortar - also preparing timber at V.21.a. 7.9. for erection of Pill Box on Canal plank. Capt. E.T. INGLEBY proceeds to U.K. on leave.	
—	14/6/18		Work continued as above. Also preparing ventilators for Mine Reservoir from (BUSNETTES. Steam Company to Bridge at V.13.a. 7.9. (14" inch.) Enemy generally shelling people & attacking up road in Loos & system in	
—	15/6/18		W.2.d. Enemy Garnering for Vicinity. Sheets of same & came Bank.	
—	16/6/18			
—	17/6/18		Lieut. R. GRIEVES joins Company from R.E. Base 14/6/18.	

Lieut. R. GRIEVES

Army Form C. 2118.

WAR DIARY
or
INTELLIGENCE SUMMARY.

(Erase heading not required)

Instructions regarding War Diaries and Intelligence Summaries are contained in F.S. Regs., Part II. and the Staff Manual respectively. Title pages will be prepared in manuscript.

Place	Date	Hour	Summary of Events and Information	Remarks and references to Appendices
BUSNETTES	18/6/18		Letter employees sent as Friendly Relief. Also wiring from Q.33.c.9.2 to	
---	19/6/18		W. + a. 2.2.	
---	20/6/18		Every C° Down to cellar at Sep C°y H.Q°.	
---	21/6/18		Every Down - from - Every through La Parisienne Line or Q.34.a.2.2 - 20/6/18.	
---	22/6/18			
---	23/6/18			
---	24/6/18		Note entrances on Lewis "Upit" Buddy Henry Street on Lamme Bank. Wiring front line 2" Upoten,	
---	25/6/18		Improving Pdt on Cannal Bank. Aspen Bog H.Q - Epinelles Aid Post at W.E.a. 1.3. that	
---	26/6/18		Reviving + sticking Camper and Kprs 2" Upotin. Post Pdn at W.2.c. 1.1. Gen'l Rivetments	
---	27/6/18		+ wiring Shelters Support Line, 1 Gpotin. Strengthening Piece Peanut Wood. Wiring front	
---	28/6/18		Q.33.D.9.2. to W. + a.2.2. Wiring Pdn 2 V.S. a.3.9. + inkering gfalls. Also Wiring Preparation Pdn at BUSHETTES (Completed) area	
---	29/6/18		in Dunkels. firing Gas Drums at Sept Coy H.Q. + Canned Bank.	
---	30/6/18		View R.G. REYES wounded 26/6/18.	
			Cent E.T. INGLEBY returned from leave to U.K. 20/6/18	
			No 490.287 Comp. Lam J. arrived the Veterinary Service Dease on Kps.	
			Directly General Departures.	
			Strength of Company 30/6/18 :- 6 officers 205 other ranks.	

Ernest Ingleby, Capt. RE
Lt 96526, Durham Forces Coy RE

War Diary.

of

The Officer Commanding 526th (Durham) Field Company R.E.

From 1st July to 31st July 1918.

Army Form C. 2118.

WAR DIARY
or
INTELLIGENCE SUMMARY.
(Erase heading not required.)

Instructions regarding War Diaries and Intelligence Summaries are contained in F.S. Regs., Part II. and the Staff Manual respectively. Title pages will be prepared in manuscript.

Place	Date	Hour	Summary of Events and Information	Remarks and references to Appendices
BUSNETTES	1/7/18		Strength of Company on 1st Monday :- 6 officers, 205 o.r.	
"	2/7/18		Section employed as follows :- Using CHEVAUX DE FRISE in CROSS ROADS, wiring from Q.23.a.9.2 to W.4.a.2.2. Temporary CHEVAUX DE FRISE for Rest Headquarters at W.2.d.4.4. and watering to same F.1 Ligne. Revetting & Strengthening Support Line. Cleaning & repairing trench at CAMEL ROADS. M.G. Emplacements at Q.32.4.5.2. Dugout Stand at V.2. a. 3.9. Laying Sgts. Racing to M.G. Emplacements at Q.37.d.5.7. Also Rue Bourgueles & R.A.P at W.6.a.1.7. CAMELLE Shellrines filling & Sanitarius.	
"	3/7/18			
"	4/7/18			
"	5/7/18			
"	6/7/18		Casualties for 1 week:- 2nd Lieut A. HUGHES. Sickness in action.	
			No. 40 281. Corpl. T. CARSON. M.M. Wounded in action (Piece of Shrapnel 4/7/18).	
			Officers Commd. of Company 2/7/18 – Capt E.T. INGLEBY R.E. Left over	
			Lieut D.A. ROBERTS. R.E. proceeded on leave to U.K. on 5/7/18 – Relieved of same 6/7/18 – 20/7/18.	
"	7/7/18		Section employed as Station above – also working & fixing the Iron Doors of Big Hd'qrs of M.G.C. –	
"	8/7/18		Revetting Shelter Gitter at BUSNETTES. Clearing Trenches & repairing and moving Iron Liners 2nd	
"	9/7/18		Leading (on 6th Inst). Reuse at BATH KILLERS. Revetting & repairing Great Roads at	
"	10/7/18		CANTRAINNE.	
			2/Lt. Leslie Levenston to Test Rivets at CANTRAINNE RE Dump Company for Canal M. 8/7/18.	
			2nd Lieut H. CHURCH R.E. joined Company from R.E. Base 10/7/18.	
"	11/7/18		Section employed on Early Land Lines & Trench CAMEL ROADS, Allied Rest Billets, R.A.P at	
"	12/7/18		W.6.d.1.7. Wiring from Q.36.o.c.2. to W.3.L.3.7. Revetting, repairing, Strengthening Support.	
"	13/7/18		M.G. Emplacements (Cheveaux - Frise) at Q.32.d.5.2. with wiring to same. Erecting	
"	14/7/18		Bath Huts at W.2.b.4.4. CHEVAUX Check for Lignes. Water Hole at BUSNETTES. Bath at	
"	15/7/18		KILLERS. Repairing dudences & laying up of M.G. Emplacement TWIN FARM at W.6.1.9.2.	
"	16/7/18		Party nearly - Repairing meeting of Shelter to Artillery at different Reservoirs (from 12 water).	
			Returning Road at BUSNETTES & Back at KILLERS. Cinders at 125 water.	
			General deceration for M.G. Emplant (near Cesin) at Q.33.d.7.4. (127 water).	
			2/Lt. Leslie relieved by 2/Lt. Leslie on forward work on 14/7/18 – 2/Lt. Leslie took over	
"	17/7/18		Rear Back at CANTRAINNE meadow by 2/Lt. Leslie.	

Army Form C. 2118.

WAR DIARY
or
INTELLIGENCE SUMMARY.
(Erase heading not required)

Instructions regarding War Diaries and Intelligence Summaries are contained in F. S. Regs., Part II. and the Staff Manual respectively. Title pages will be prepared in manuscript.

Place	Date	Hour	Summary of Events and Information	Remarks and references to Appendices
ROSIETTES.	18/7/18		Sections employed as detailed for M'wind v'onade - also Supervising reparations for Cheval at Tm. Bat. HQ. Sec. employed at Spaine Dump, Siding to Cheval Reveler etc.	
	19/7/18		Repairs to Company Billets. Work on Rose Demolition v Bridge there etc.	
	20/7/18		On 19" wind - firing charge there etc. Casualties :- 18/7/18 - No. 13558 Sapper TURNER. H. Sickness in Action 18/7/18	
	24/7/18		No. 135578 Sapper TURNER. H. Sickness in Action 18/7/18	
			2nd Section relieves No 2 Section on forward work. 20/7/18. No 2 Section take over Eye Back at Contrainne. Commence by Not Section.	
27/4/18			Capt. T. W. NOTTRES R.E. takes off Charge of Company. Transferred to England. 14/7/18 - Authority :- List No. 1195 dated 19/7/18 v Subur "A" to M. 129/2 Get dated 22/7/18.	
23/7/18			Section employed on above dudge - also Commence laying Site for 2nd are Camp by Rose Hole v Pigeon Farm. Guarrung, Breakwork to form two Breastwork Support Line	
24/7/18			Party assisting 4 Australian Tunnelling Coy, 148 (Supr) the Ed Ex in 22/7/18.	
25/7/18			Making new work from Comml time.	
26/4/18			Capt. S NORTH R.E. Junior Coy in Command 25/7/18 for advancement of all work.	
			No. 2 Section relieves No. 3 Section on forward work on 26/7/18. No. 3 Section take over Eye Buret at Contrainne commenced by No. 2 Section.	
27/7/18			Section employed on duties as above - also Smoking Orange Shelleing v Come Bards	
28/7/18			Entrance Dugout in Renue Burt, Eight Railway 4 Sand.	
29/7/18			MAJOR G.F. HALL R.E. Joined Company from R.E. Base Depot on 3/7/18 v assumes	
30/7/18			Supervising Infantry in wiring.	
31/7/18			Command of Company.	

Strength of Company on 31/7/18 :- 6 Officers 207. other ranks.

P.H. Hall
Major R.E.
526. (Sunderland) Field Company R.E.

War Diary.

of

"The Officer Commanding 526th (Durham) Siege Company R.E.

From 1st August to 31st August 1918

WAR DIARY or INTELLIGENCE SUMMARY

Army Form C. 2118.

(Erase heading not required.)

Place	Date	Hour	Summary of Events and Information	Remarks and references to Appendices
BUSNETTES	1/8/18		Strength of Company 1/8/18 :- 6 Officers, 207 Other ranks.	
"	2/8/18		Section employed as follows:- Construction of breastwork shelter at Pacaut Farm. Construction of breastwork supported line in Rifle & Left of Pacaut Wood. Wiring	
"	3/8/18		Enemy very demonstrative. New breastwork support line in Rifle & left of Pacaut Wood. Wiring Traverse in to system. Repair to R.A.P. W.2.d.6.t.1. Block enemy bridge	
"	4/8/18		M.G. emplacement on left of Pacaut Wood (Block) on Canal Bank. Blair Pellos (M.G. Emplacement) Progress on 2/8/18.	
"	5/8/18		Enemy bridge (Block) on Canal Bank. Blair Pellos (M.G. Emplacement) & Contraigne E. Extensions	
"	6/8/18		M.G. emplacement at Lone House.	
"	7/8/18		Wiring & divertery railway on Chelsea Bridge on 7/8/18.	
"	8/8/18		at Contraigne same day. No 1 Section relieves No 1 Section at Embrasure works on 11/8/18. No 1 Section took over Lone Post No 1 Section relieves No 1 Section on same work on 7/8/18. No 1 Section took over Lone Post	
"	8/8/18		at Contraigne same day. Construction of breastworks. Canal Bank.	
"	9/8/18		Section employed on work as follows:- R.A.P. at Pacaut Farm. Relieved to M.G. Dugout at Lone House. More Pierre in support line. Myler Tracks from Bridge on W.3.T. 6.5. to Lone Bank Q.33.e.3.2 to Q.27.a.2.6 and from R.A.P. to Lone Bank. Post taken over from Lone Bridge at Contraigne on 7/8/18. No 2 Section moves up to Hill Farm.	
"	10/8/18		Section employed as follows:- Enemy Post taken over at embrasure Post No 1 at Q.34.a.9.2. Clearing breastwork in Pacaut Wood. Enemy defensive firing stand at Contraigne. Extension of	
"	11/8/18		over the trenches as ft. 1 wide etc. Wiring in Pacaut Wood.	
"	12/8/18		II Lieut. S.S. PARKES joins company from R.E. Base on 10/8/18.	
"	13/8/18			
"	14/8/18		Work on village above, also employed taking guns at Hill at Q.3d. & 7.5.60. & firing trench Brests. Entry English track at Burres Farm. Commence nearly Moire Pierre at W.4a.4.5.	
"	15/8/18		on 17/8/18. Opening up Rails Point at Q.29.a.85.60 on 20/8/18.	
"	16/8/18		No 3 Section moved up to GORNEHEM on 17/8/18.	
"	17/8/18		Do Do " " " 18/8/18	
GORNEHEM	18/8/18		Do Do " " " 19/8/18	
"	19/8/18		Coy. & No 1 " " " "	
"	20/8/18		No 1 & 3 Section moved back to BUSNETTES on 21/8/18	
"	21/8/18			

Army Form C. 2118.

WAR DIARY
or
INTELLIGENCE SUMMARY.
(Erase heading not required.)

Instructions regarding War Diaries and Intelligence Summaries are contained in F.S. Regs., Part II. and the Staff Manual respectively. Title pages will be prepared in manuscript.

Place	Date	Hour	Summary of Events and Information	Remarks and references to Appendices
GOUY-EN-HEM.	22/8/18		Section employed as follows:- Superintending horse system. Come Const. Horse lines, Support line. Infantry Supply lines from Chelsea Bridge to G.29.a. 9.4. Trekking R.E. unloading into 3 dumps on Command Roads. Refering Route CONTRAINNE.	
BUSNETTES.	23/8/18		H.Q. + Nos. 2 + 4 Sections returned to BUSNETTES 22/8/18.	
RELY.	24/8/18		Company moved from BUSNETTES to RELY.	
TERNAS.	25/8/18		Mounted Section bivouaced by march route at 7.0 p.m. 24/8/18. From RELY en route for TERNAS. Dismounted personnel moved from RELY at 6 a.m. 25/8/18 - marched to LILLERS - entrained LILLERS + detrained at BRYAS + marched to TERNAS.	
BOUVIGNY.	26/8/18		Company moved by march route at 6 p.m. from TERNAS to BOUVIGNY.	
(BOIS-de-BOUVIGNY)	27/8/18		Company moved into BOIS-de-BOUVIGNY.	
HAPPY-VALLEY.	28/8/18		Company moved from BOIS-de-BOUVIGNY. Mounted Section by march route to ARRAS - Dismounted Section by Buses to HAPPY VALLEY, E. of ARRAS.	
	29/8/18		No. 1 Sect. reconnaissance forward points - No. 2 & No. 3 repair fords - No. 4 in reserve.	
	30/8/18		To trestles N. of MONCHY. Work as yesterday, No. 3 in reserve. At night all sections except No. 1 bridging the SENSEE river between REMY and the ARRAS-CAMBRAI road - HQ pioneers carrying party.	
	31/8/18		Moved camp to French near BOIS DU VERT. No. 2 & No. 1 bridging SENSEE river N. of REMY. No. 3 developing water supply in BOIRY. No. 4 in reserve. Strength of Company 31/8/18 :- 7 Officers 204 other ranks.	

J. Mallaby. R.E.
Colin 5H Co. R.E.
5/9/18.

War Diary.

of

The Officer Commanding 526th (Durham) Field Company R.E.

From 1st September to 30th September 1918.

Army Form C. 2118.

WAR DIARY
or
INTELLIGENCE SUMMARY.

(Erase heading not required.)

Instructions regarding War Diaries and Intelligence Summaries are contained in F. S. Regs., Part II. and the Staff Manual respectively. Title pages will be prepared in manuscript.

Place	Date	Hour	Summary of Events and Information	Remarks and references to Appendices
WOOD NEAR BOIS du VERT	1/9/18	-	Strength Section 1/9/18 :- Officer 2 O.R. 105. Section employed as follows :- One Section Offr: Remaining ORs Remainder digging by No.2 & 3 Section moved to REMY at midnight. 519503 Spr PHILLIPS G.F. admitted 1/9/18 BOISY.	
REMY	2/9/18	-	No.1 Section moved to REMY at 4 a.m. Nos.1,2,3 Section repairing + maintaining various Roads from Cam to Rail in neighbourhood of REMY & ETERPIGNY.	
"	3/9/18		No.1 Section developing water supply in ETERPIGNY. No.2 " " " " making road diversion in ETERPIGNY & repairing bridge in ETERPIGNY. No.3 " " " " Repairing roads in vicinity of ETERPIGNY. Company relieved at 10 p.m. by 23rd (Welsh) Company RE. & moved to billets in neighbourhood of FOSSES CAVES. Casualties :- 285177 Spr. CADMAN J.A.] 471311 " EMMERSON R.] admitted 2/9/18. 471257 " DUNCAN G.]	
MINGOVAL	4/9/18	-	Dismounted personnel moved by Bus to MINGOVAL. Mounted Section moved to MINGOVAL by march route.	
"	5/9/18		Inspection of personnel, equipment, Tool Carts, + Mules.	
"	6/9/18		Company + Section Drill.	
"	7/9/18		Bath.	
"	8/9/18		Company Sports.	
"	9/9/18		Lieut. A.T. CODLING proceeded on leave to UK 11/9/18. Lieut RE. MILES rejoined from France 11/9/18.	
"	10/9/18			
"	11/9/18			
"	12/9/18			
"	13/9/18			
"	14/9/18			
"	15/9/18			
"	16/9/18			
"	17/9/18			
"	18/9/18			

Army Form C. 2118.

WAR DIARY
or
INTELLIGENCE SUMMARY.
(Erase heading not required.)

Instructions regarding War Diaries and Intelligence
Summaries are contained in F. S. Regs., Part II.
and the Staff Manual respectively. Title pages
will be prepared in manuscript.

Place	Date	Hour	Summary of Events and Information	Remarks and references to Appendices
MONCHY (vicinity) Sheet 51.b. O.7.a.O.8.	19/9/18		Company moved from MIRVOUX to O.7.a. O.8. (near MONCHY). Remainder Personnel by train & dismounted stables by road route to N.14.b.67. O.7. stabler to BOIRY.	
	20/9/18		Company employed as follows: – Maintaining Lyer Bridge between MONCHY & BOIRY. Clearing 3 tunnels in Dump at N.15.a.5.9. Reconnaissance for supply of BOIRY, PELVES, Clearing tunnels in Bank at FRESNEY (H.24.a. "MONCHY")	
	21/9/18		Clearing underground feature. Fire fairing. Clearing wells, establishing water supply at PELVES, MONCHY & BOIRY, Supply Dump – improving & clearing roads in BOIRY – ARRAS. O.1. a.16, O.1.a.61, Trench Park & Fresent Improvement	
	22/9/18		Party of 1960 O.Rs attached to Div. Details LOUEZ for work (24/9/18).	
	23/9/18			
	24/9/18			
	25/9/18		Work carrying as above also improving Divn. accommodation at Bois Hall (Rannes) & Ball Helm. Repairing Railway Bridge & O.S. at 4 & Fifty Cor. Curtain to Airey Dugout. Fire fairing Excavation from BOIRY to I.32.d.1.6. Trench Park	
	26/9/18		at O.3. a.1.8. Repairs to Baths at 12th Diesel Ambulance.	
	27/9/18		Commenced improvements to Divisional Headquarters at	
	28/9/18		Les Fosse Farm, on 30/9/18.	
	29/9/18		Lieut. A. T. Coding rejoined from Leave 28/9/18.	
	30/9/18		Strength of Company 30/9/18 :– 7 Officers 198 O.Rs.	

Kenneth Inglesby
Capt. R.E.

1st/653rd (Durham) Field Company R.E.

War Diary - Lt. Col. (Renfrew) Field Coy. R.E.

406TH
(RENFREW)
FIELD COMPANY, R.E.
October 1918

War Diary

of

The Officer Commanding 526" (Durham) Field Company R.E.

From 1st October to 31st October 1918.

Army Form C. 2118.

WAR DIARY
or
INTELLIGENCE SUMMARY.
(Erase heading not required.)

Instructions regarding War Diaries and Intelligence Summaries are contained in F. S. Regs., Part II. and the Staff Manual respectively. Title pages will be prepared in manuscript.

Place	Date	Hour	Summary of Events and Information	Remarks and references to Appendices
NOEUX (Mines) Sheet 51B O.7.a.0.8	1/10/18		Strength of Company 1/10/18 :- 7 officers 178 other ranks. Company employed as follows: Railway from BOIRY to T.32.a.4.8. Pit head phone trunk. Maintaining Lighting from BOIRY any RALINES. Extending Artillery phone in fifteen up dugout shaft. 7 filling ¾ in cartridges to charge 2 at O.3.d. 20.50, O.9.a.11.71. at O.5.d. 30.20. Trench catwalks, trucks & general internment & equipment at Brigade stores.	
""	2/10/18		Employed as above. Inspired accommodation at Riencourt.	
""	3/10/18		Major G.F. HALL proceeded on leave to PARIS. 1/10/18. Capt. E.J. INGLESBY	
""	4/10/18		proceeded in same to PARIS. 1/10/18.	
""	5/10/18		Lieut. DA ROBERTS to R.E. School ROUEN – Course 3/10/18.
""	6/10/18		Company Commander of Company. 1/10/18. The Stirling Nature – vide & Orders 1/10/18. Lieut WILDE. H. Assumes Company Commander. 1/10/18
			No. 546911 L/Cpl. WILDE. H.	
DAINVILLE	7/10/18		Company moved by trucks route to DAINVILLE.	
""	8/10/18		Inspection of Cabling, regiments etc.	
""	9/10/18		Gentlemen of Welcom trestle disc.	
""	10/10/18		Major G.F. HALL rejoined from PARIS leave. Lieut. Wilson trestle disc. II Lieut. Clever. Rains C/CD. nicolas Bridge. Construction at MARQUION. Lieut A.J. CODLING. proceeded to Empire Road	
BOURLON WOOD (Vicinity)	11/10/18		Company march to vicinity of BOURLON WOOD. Advanced HQ by Bus to FONTAINE NOTRE DAME. Organized Advance by Coys route lorry for night 11/12 Det at WANCOURT continued move of 12" Bed.	
""	12/10/18		Improving accommodation vicinity.	
ESCAUDOEUVRES	13/10/18		Company moved by trucks route to ESCAUDOEUVRES.	

Army Form C. 2118.

WAR DIARY
or
INTELLIGENCE SUMMARY.
(Erase heading not required.)

Place	Date	Hour	Summary of Events and Information	Remarks and references to Appendices
ESCAUDOEUVRES	14/10/18		Company employed repairing roads &c in ESCAUDOEUVRES.	
"	15/10/18		Section employed clearing roadway & demolished railway bridge at T.11.a.2.2.	
"	16/10/18		Section employed clearing roadway at demolished railway bridge at T.11.b.2.5.	
"	17/10/18		Section employed making deviation round from T.11.a.8.8. to T.11.d.35. v T.11.c.2.9.	
NAVES.	18/10/18		Company Head Quarters moved from ESCAUDOEUVRES to NAVES. Major G.F. Hall R.E. proceeded to U.K. - Capt. I.E.T. INGLEBY R.E. assumed temporary command of Company.	
"	19/10/18		Section employed erecting H. footbridge (24 ft span) v I.footbridge (15 ft span) - these bridges to span river & other channels to AVESNES-LE-SEC at night. No 2 Section moved forward to AVESNES-LE-SEC.	
"	20/10/18		No 2 Section - operation by Infantry Carrying parties attacking troops v these infantry carrying bridges with river SENSÉE.	
			From SENSÉE reconnaissance for position of light truss Bridge to take 1st Line Transport and Ambulance bridges at HASPRES at P.13.a.0.4. v P.13.a.3.5. investigations & report made as to replacement of heavy truss bridges. No 3 Section moved forward to AVESNES-LE-SEC.	
AVESNES-LE-SEC.	21/10/18		Headquarters v Nos. 1 v 4 Sections moved to AVESNES-LE-SEC. Sections employed erecting truss bridges at P.13.c.0.4. v P.13.a.3.5. making deviations & approaches. Clearing away debris of demolished bridges & repairing approaches to Heavy truss Bridge.	
			Reconnaissance v report made of demolished railway bridge at HASPRES at P.13.a.5.6 v P.13.a.8.2. report made on zine turning at P.13.a.5.2. Inspection of the approach to twenty arch bridge to be partly interfered by tunnelling by R.E.	
"	22/10/18		Nos. 1 & 3 Sections moved to HASPRES. Sections employed in preparation of roadway v foundations of piers for the 2 heavy truss	

Army Form C. 2118.

WAR DIARY
or
INTELLIGENCE SUMMARY.

(Erase heading not required.)

Instructions regarding War Diaries and Intelligence Summaries are contained in F.S. Regs., Part II. and the Staff Manual respectively. Title pages will be prepared in manuscript.

Place	Date	Hour	Summary of Events and Information	Remarks and references to Appendices
AVESNES-LE SEC	23/10/18		Nos 2 & 4 Sections moved to HASPRES. HASPRES. Continues work on Heavy Girder Bridge at HASPRES. Nos 23rd/24th Oct. Section Offr 3. 4 moves forward to Check Rd at P.13. 2.3.7. v 2 Trestle Bridges taken to same place to avoid next time in morning of 24th inst unless skly order to forward to erect the Bridge.	
HASPRES	24/10/18		Trestle Bridges erected on River ECAILLON at P.4. a. 2.8. v T. 34. a. 1.1. Company HQrs moves to HASPRES.	
"	25/10/18		Section employes as follows:- Maintaining Bridges on River ECAILLON. Improving approaches to Heavy Bridge at MONCHAUX (T.34. a. 1.3). Repairing road HASPRES - SAULZOIR. Lt Gen. G.E.H. WILSON. R.E. James Company from R.E. Base Depot.	
"	26/10/18		Nos 1 & 4 Sections moves to MONCHAUX. v employes repairing road MONCHAUX - VERCHAIN between T 33. d. 4. 1 - P.10. a. 4. 8. Also recovering Clandestine German Trestle Bridge at T. 34. a. 2. 9. Nos 2 v 3 Sections employes making 6 Trestle Bridges. Taking down Trestle Bridges at HASPRES (P.13. a. 1.4) v relative approaches. Opening Charing road. Nos 26/27th Oct. 4 footbridges put in at K. 29. a. 2. 8.	
"	27/10/18		Section employes Channeling Trestle Bridge over River SELLE at P.19.a.6.7. - Treating approaches v transporting Cans to Bg HQrs. Maintaining v improving East Bridge at ARTRES. Lieut RE MILES, M.C. R.E. to England. Lieut RE MILES, M.C. R.E. to England for transfer to R.A.F.	

(A7092) Wt. W12899/M1293 75 ,o.o. 1/17. D. D. & L., Ltd. Forms/C2118/14.

WAR DIARY
or
INTELLIGENCE SUMMARY.
(Erase heading not required.)

Army Form C. 2118.

Place	Date	Hour	Summary of Events and Information	Remarks and references to Appendices
HASPRES	28/10/18		{ No. 2 & 3 Section moved to QUERSNAING & employed preparing accommodation for 11th Inf Brigade.	
	29/10/18		No. 1 Section maintaining Bridges in ESCANION & RHONELLE. No. 1 Section making. No. 3 Section returned to HASPRES in 29th inst.	
"	30/10/18		Sections employed as follows:- Strengthening & improving ADS at QUERSNAING. Improving approaches of heavy Bridges at MONCHAUX. Making superstructure for heavy Bridge to stock. Reconnaissance of Fosse RHONELLE between K.29.a. 3.8 & K.22.d. 7.2 with view to bridging for 1st Line transport & Field Guns.	
"	31/10/18		Sections employed as follows:- Erected Trestle Bridge over Fosse RHONELLE at K.23.c.0.0. between 2 buildings all Fosse RHONELLE between K.22.a. 8.5 and K.22.d. 8.8. Capt. R.W. MITCHELL M.C. R.E. joined from 412 Field Company R.E. and assumed command of Company.	

Strength of Company 31/10/18 :- 7 Officers + 202 other ranks.

Ernest Taylor, Capt. R.E.
O/C 526 (Ontario) Field Company R.E.

War Diary

of

The Officer Commanding, 526th (Durham) Field Company R.E.

"From 1st November to 30th November 1918."

Army Form C. 2118.

WAR DIARY
or
INTELLIGENCE SUMMARY.
(Erase heading not required.)

Instructions regarding War Diaries and Intelligence Summaries are contained in F. S. Regs., Part II. and the Staff Manual respectively. Title pages will be prepared in manuscript.

Place	Date	Hour	Summary of Events and Information	Remarks and references to Appendices
HASPRES.	1/11/18		Strength Monday 1st November 1918:- 7 Officers, 202 other ranks. Company Headquarters at HASPRES. No 1 & 4 Section at MONCHAUX. No 2 Section at QUERENAING. No 3 Section at HASPRES. Planned section at AVESNES-LE-SEC. Section employed as follows:- Building 2 trestle bridge for lorry transport over HONDELLE RIVER. 1 commenced at 2cm. (?) 1 commenced at 3pm. (?) 2pm & 4pm. Erecting footbridges for infantry.	
"	2/11/18		No 2 Section moved to HASPRES. Trestle bridges by MONCHAUX Commenced.	
"	3/11/18		No 1 & 4 Section returned to HASPRES. Trestle Bridge at MONCHAUX Completed.	
MAING	4/11/18		Company moved from HASPRES to MAING.	
"	5/11/18		Section Commander started on road repairs at 12 noon on road from MAING to 600 yards E. of FAMARS including demolished Railway Bridge at K.13 & 7.4. Making good same.	
"	6/11/18		Work continues on road repairs. Lieut. D. A. ROBERTS rejoined company from R.E. Base Rouen 6/11/18.	
"	7/11/18		Lieut. AT. CODLING rejoined company from Casualty 5/11/18. Seconded to Divisional Engineer Coy. to injuring.	
"	8/11/18		Available personnel to 4137 Field Coy. RE. No 1 & 3 Section employed on road repair. No 2 & 4 " " on training.	
SEBOURG.	9/11/18		Company moved from MAING to SEBOURG. T/Lieut. F.H.B. YERBURY joined company from R.E. Base Depot.	
AUDREGNIES (BELGIUM)	10/11/18		Company moved from SEBOURG to AUDREGNIES. 2/C 40216, L/Cpl. JAGGE.T. awarded the Military Medal. 2/C 470058. Sapp. McCLARY.S. " "	
"	11/11/18		Section commenced work building Heavy Bridge at AUDREGNIES (T.G. A. Central)	

Army Form C. 2118.

WAR DIARY
or
INTELLIGENCE SUMMARY.
(Erase heading not required.)

Instructions regarding War Diaries and Intelligence Summaries are contained in F. S. Regs., Part II. and the Staff Manual respectively. Title pages will be prepared in manuscript.

Place	Date	Hour	Summary of Events and Information	Remarks and references to Appendices
AUDREGNIES.	12/11/18		Work continues on Henry Bridge — stones for traffic.	
"	13/11/18		Section employed Completing Henry Bridge. Washing transport.	
"	14/11/18		Section employed improving Henry Bridge. Washing transport.	
"	15/11/18		Strenae Drive & Section & Company Drive.	
"	16/11/18		Physical Drill. Section Drive & Rifle Exercise. Lecture by O.C. on "Sportsmanship & Demobilization".	No. 4710.52. Lofbop Bde F. Annual Training Issued.
"	17/11/18		Company move Cancelled. Company Drill afternoon.	
"	18/11/18		Physical Drill. Rifle Exercise. Lecture Drill. Lecture by H.O.B. to 3/6 Company on "Sportsmanship & Demobilization". Educational Classes commenced.	
CURGIES. (FRANCE)	19/11/18		Company moved from AUDREGNIES to CURGIES. Divisional G.O.C. inspects troops of Division at 1030 hours.	
SAULTAIN.	20/11/18		Company moved from CURGIES to SAULTAIN in afternoon.	
"	21/11/18		Section & Company Drive. Technical Classes.	
"	22/11/18		Section & Company Drive & Technical Classes. Transport of Division inspected by G.O.C. Division at 1030 hours.	
"	23/11/18		Section & Company Drive & Educational Classes.	
"	24/11/18		Church Parade. Lecture by M.O. in afternoon on Venereal Disease.	
"	25/11/18		Grand Washing Drive. Washing transport. Lieut. S.S. PARKES proceeds on leave from 2 to U.K.	

Army Form C. 2118.

WAR DIARY
or
INTELLIGENCE SUMMARY.
(Erase heading not required.)

Instructions regarding War Diaries and Intelligence Summaries are contained in F. S. Regs., Part II. and the Staff Manual respectively. Title pages will be prepared in manuscript.

Place	Date	Hour	Summary of Events and Information	Remarks and references to Appendices
SAULTY HUTS.	26/11/18		Section employed clearing transport & Coulverine Lines.	
"	27/11/18		Captain E.T. INGLEBY proceed on leave to U.K.	
"	28/11/18		Section Rains & Grave Mounting. Coulverine Lines.	
"	28/11/18		Corps of Armies inspected by 1st Army Commander. – Company represented by party of 60 other ranks.	
"	29/11/18		Section Rains & Grave Mounting etc. Coulverine Lines.	
"	29/11/18		Grave Mounting Rains & Coulverine fatigues.	
			Strength of Company 30 November 1918:- 7 officers, 192 other ranks.	

R. Mitchell
Major C.E.
O.C. 256" (Durham) Tunnel Company R.E.

War Diary

of

The Officer Commanding 526th (Durham) Field Company R.E.

From 1st December to 31st December 1918.

Army Form C. 2118.

WAR DIARY
or
INTELLIGENCE SUMMARY.
(Erase heading not required.)

Instructions regarding War Diaries and Intelligence Summaries are contained in F. S. Regs., Part II. and the Staff Manual respectively. Title pages will be prepared in manuscript.

Place	Date	Hour	Summary of Events and Information	Remarks and references to Appendices
SAULTAIN	1/12/16		Strength of Company 1st December 1916 :– 7 Officers & 192 other ranks.	
"	2/12/16		Church Parade. Each Parade.	
"	3/12/16		Lectures, Discs & Gun mounting. Educational Classes.	
"	4/12/16		Musketry (30 yds range). Lectures, Discs & Gun mounting. Educational Classes.	
"	5/12/16			
"	6/12/16			
"	7/12/16		1st Infantry Brigade inspected by Brigadier General Commanding Allenby's Dismounts parade.	
"	8/12/16		Church Parade.	
"	9/12/16		Musketry (30 yds range). Lectures Discs & Gun mounting. Educational Classes.	
"	10/12/16		Coys Commander presented medal ribbons to Officers, NCOs & men of 1st Infantry Brigade Reported from this Company :– No 470216 S.Q.M.S. Hopes L Hickey Wine No 471052 Sergeant Bell W. Capt. No 546911 Capt Miles G.H.	
"	11/12/16			
"	12/12/16			
"	13/12/16		Church Parade. Demobilization of Officers Commenced. Lectures Discs & Guns Mounting. 16th Class.	
"	14/12/16		Musketry (30 yds range). Educational Classes.	
"	15/12/16		Lieut L.J. Parkes returned from Leave 13/12/16.	
"	16/12/16			
"	17/12/16		Church Parade. Capt. E.J. INGLEBY from Leave	

(A7592) Wt W12839/M1293 75,000 1/17. D.D. & L., Ltd. Forms/C2118/24.

Army Form C. 2118.

WAR DIARY
or
INTELLIGENCE SUMMARY
(Erase heading not required.)

Instructions regarding War Diaries and Intelligence Summaries are contained in F.S. Regs., Part II. and the Staff Manual respectively. Title pages will be prepared in manuscript.

Place	Date	Hour	Summary of Events and Information	Remarks and references to Appendices
SAULTAIN	16/10/18		Fatigues. Lewis Gun Instruction (1960 "Loos" fr Lewin) Educational Class.	
"	17/10/18		Gas Class. Lewis Gun Instruction. Educational Class.	
"	18/10/18		T/Lieut Rhodes proceeded on leave to U.K. attached to 10th Bn L. Inf.	
"	19/10/18		N.C.O.'s & Sots. Dance. to Hospital.	
"	20/10/18		Demonstration of Musketry practice in CHAMPS DE TIR Gorge. Physical Training & Bayonet Fighting Exercise. Lewis Gun Instruction. Lecture. Capt. F.T.INGLEBY	
			Quiz. Educational Class. N.C.O. Class. Lewis Gun Leave to U.K. (20/10/18)	
"	21/10/18		Major R.W.MITCHELL M.C. R.E. Resumed Temporary Command of Company.	
"	22/10/18		Boss Parade.	
"	23/10/18		Church Parade.	
"	24/10/18		Physical Training & Bayonet Fighting Exercise. Lewis Gun Instruction. Lecture.	
"	25/10/18		Quiz. N.C.O. Class. Educational Class.	
"	26/10/18		Church Parade. Company Christmas Dinner Concert.	
"	27/10/18		Boxing. Lewis Gun Instruction. Lecture. Once. N.C.O. Class	
"	28/10/18		Physical Training & Bayonet Fighting Exercise. Lecture Once.	
"	29/10/18		Educational Class.	
"	30/10/18		Church Parade. N.C.O. Class. Educational Class.	
"	31/10/18		Lewis Gun Instruction. Lecture Once. Strength of Company 31/10/18:- Officers 7 other ranks 179.	

Arnold J. Inglesby Capt GE
for O/C 56th (Durham) Salva Coy. RE

War Diary

of

The Officer Commanding. 526th (Durham) Field Coy R.E

From 1st January to 31st January. 1919.

Army Form C. 2118.

WAR DIARY
or
INTELLIGENCE SUMMARY.
(Erase heading not required)

Instructions regarding War Diaries and Intelligence Summaries are contained in F. S. Regs., Part II. and the Staff Manual respectively. Title pages will be prepared in manuscript.

Place	Date	Hour	Summary of Events and Information	Remarks and references to Appendices
SAULTAIN.	1-1-19		Strength of Coy: 1st January 1919 7 Officers + 179 O.R. in Ranks	
"	2-1-19		Church Parade for Roman Catholics. Kit Parade.	
"			Physical Drill & Lewis Gun Instruction.	
"			Educational Classes.	
"	3-1-19		Physical Drill & Lewis Gun Instruction.	
"			Educational Classes.	
"	4-1-19		Mounted Section and Transport moved from SAULTAIN to MORLANWELZ.	
"			Dismounted Section. Physical Training & Lewis Gun Instruction.	
"			Educational Classes.	
"	5-1-19		Dismounted Section moved from SAULTAIN to MORLANWELZ.	
MORLANWELZ (BELGIUM)	6-1-19		Fatigues.	
"	7-1-19		Physical Drill, Section Drill and Educational Classes.	
"			2/Lieut G.E.H. Wilson proceeded to U.K. on Leave. (7-1-19)	
"	8-1-19		Physical Drill and Section Drill, and Educational classes.	
"	9-1-19		Inspection of 's company by 2/Capt C.J. Ingleby R.E. acting o/c.	
"	10-1-19			
"	11-1-19		} Physical Drill. Section Drill and Educational classes.	
"	12-1-19		Church Parade.	
"	13-1-19		Physical Drill and Inspection at Company by Capt C.J. Ingleby acting o/c.	
"	14-1-19		} Physical Drill. Section Drill and Educational Classes.	
"	15-1-19			

Army Form C. 2118.

WAR DIARY
or
INTELLIGENCE SUMMARY.
(Erase heading not required.)

Instructions regarding War Diaries and Intelligence Summaries are contained in F. S. Regs., Part II. and the Staff Manual respectively. Title pages will be prepared in manuscript.

Places	Date	Hour	Summary of Events and Information	Remarks and references to Appendices
MORLANWELZ	16-1-19		Physical Drill, Section Drill and Educational Classes.	
"	17-1-19		2/Lt S.S. PARKES evacuated to England (sick) 17.1.19.	
"	18-1-19		Inspection of Company by 2nd Lt. C. C. Johnson D.S.O.R.E. 18 A.T. 4th Division.	
"	19-1-19		Church Parade.	
"	20-1-19		Physical Drill, Section Drill and Educational Classes.	
"	21-1-19		F.H.B. Johnson to Hospital (Sick) 20/1/19. Major R.W. Mitchell M.C. R.E. returned from leave to U.K. and resumed command of Company.	
"	22-1-19		Physical Drill, Section Drill and Educational Classes.	
"	23-1-19		2nd Lieut B.E.H. Hilton returned from leave to U.K.	
"	24-1-19		Physical Drill, Section Drill and Educational Classes.	
"	25-1-19			
"	26-1-19		Church Parade.	
"	27-1-19		Physical Drill, Section Drill, Lewis Gun Instruction and Educational Classes.	
"	28-1-19			
"	29-1-19		Lieut G. A. Roberts proceeded on leave to U.K. 30/1/19.	
"	30-1-19			
"	31-1-19		Physical Drill, Section Drill and Educational Classes and Lewis Gun Instruction.	

Strength of Company 31-1-19. 5 Officers. & 134 Other Ranks.

R.W. Mitchell Major R.E.
O/C 526 Durham Field Company. R.E.

War Diary

of

The Officer Commanding 526 (Durham) Field Coy. R.E.

From February 1st to February 28th 1919.

Army Form C. 2118.

WAR DIARY
INTELLIGENCE SUMMARY.
(Erase heading not required.)

Instructions regarding War Diaries and Intelligence Summaries are contained in F. S. Regs., Part II. and the Staff Manual respectively. Title pages will be prepared in manuscript.

Place	Date	Hour	Summary of Events and Information	Remarks and references to Appendices
MORLANWELZ	1-2-19		Strength of Company February 1st 1919 5 Officers & 134 ORs	
			Fatigue etc.	
	2-2-19		Church Parade.	
	3-3-19		Physical Training. Section Drill & Lewis Gun Instruction.	
			Relieved by Major R.W. MITCHELL M.C. R.E. in "Demobilization".	
	4-2-19		Physical Training. Section Drill & Lewis Gun Instruction.	
	5-2-19		Work commenced in return to Gun & man Stables at Manage.	
	6-2-19			
	7-2-19		Physical Training. Section Drill & Lewis Gun Instruction.	
	8-2-19		Fatigues etc.	
	9-2-19		Church Parade.	
	10-2-19		Physical Training. Section Drill & Lewis Gun Instruction.	
			Return to Gun & man Stables at Manage completed.	
	11-2-19		Physical Training. Sub. Drill & Lewis Gun Instruction.	
	12-2-19			
	13-2-19		Rest Parade	
	13-2-19			
	14-2-19		Physical Training. Section Drill & Lewis Gun Instruction.	
	15-2-19		Fatigues etc.	
	16-2-19		Church Parade.	

Army Form C. 2118.

Instructions regarding War Diaries and Intelligence Summaries are contained in F. S. Regs., Part II. and the Staff Manual respectively. Title pages will be prepared in manuscript.

WAR DIARY
or
INTELLIGENCE SUMMARY.
(Erase heading not required.)

Place	Date	Hour	Summary of Events and Information	Remarks and references to Appendices
MORIANWELZ	17-2-19		⎫ Physical Training. Section Drill & Lewis Gun Instruction.	
"	18-2-19		⎬ 2nd Lieut F.H.S. YERBURY evacuated to U.K. (sick).	
"	19-2-19		⎭	
"	19-2-19		⎫ Physical Training. Section Drill & Lewis Gun Instruction.	
"	20-2-19		Bath Parade.	
"	21-2-19		Physical Training. Section Drill & Lewis Gun Instruction	
"	22-2-19		Fatigues etc.	
"	23-2-19		Church Parade.	
"	23-2-19		2nd Lieut P.A. ROBERTS returned from leave to U.K.	
"	24-2-19		Physical Training. Rifle Inspection & Lewis Gun Instruction.	
"	24-2-19		Major R.W. MITCHELL M.C.R.E. assumed temporary duty of C.R.E. 4th Division	
"			Capt E. JINGLEBY R.E. assumed temporary command of Company.	
"	25-2-19		⎫ Physical Training. Section Drill & Lewis Gun Instruction.	
"	26-2-19		Bath Parade.	
"	27-2-19		⎬	
"	28-2-19		Physical Training. Section Drill & Lewis Gun Instruction.	

Strength of Company February 28-1919. 4 Officers, 90 O.R.S.

Ernest Jingleby Capt R.E.
O/C. 526th (Durham) Field Coy R.E.

www.ingramcontent.com/pod-product-compliance
Lightning Source LLC
Chambersburg PA
CBHW080905230426
43664CB00016B/2734